About the Author

Dr. Donald R. Burleson is a Field Investigator, Consultant, and Research Specialist for MUFON, the Mutual UFO Network, for which he also serves as State Director for New Mexico. An extensively published writer, he has done original research into the Roswell incident, the Lubbock Lights, the Levelland, Texas UFO landings, Socorro, and other cases, and is the author of the books *The Golden Age of UFOs* and *UFO Secrecy and the Fall of J. Robert Oppenheimer*, as well as numerous research articles published in the *MUFON UFO Journal* and the J. Allen Hynek Center for UFO Studies journal *International UFO Reporter*. He holds master's degrees in mathematics and English and a Ph.D. in English literature, and is semi-retired from the Mathematics Department at Eastern New Mexico University in Roswell, New Mexico, having taught mathematics at several other universities. He has appeared on Good Morning America, Nightline, Fox, and the History Channel, and is a frequent lecturer on topics in the field of UFO studies. He and his wife Mollie (herself a writer and fellow UFO investigator) have lived in Roswell since 1996.

Some Other Books by Donald R. Burleson:

Field of UFO Studies:

UFO Secrecy and the Fall of J. Robert Oppenheimer

Literary Criticism:

Begging to Differ: Deconstructionist Readings
Lovecraft: Disturbing the Universe
H. P. Lovecraft: A Critical Study

Novels:

Flute Song (The Roswell Crewman)
Arroyo
A Roswell Christmas Carol
A Capitalist Christmas Carol

Collections of Short Stories:

Beyond the Lamplight
Four Shadowings
Lemon Drops and Other Horrors
Wait for the Thunder

UFOs and the Murder of Marilyn Monroe

Donald R. Burleson, Ph.D.

BLACK MESA PRESS
Roswell, New Mexico
2003 / 2014

Copyright © 2003   Donald R. Burleson

Published by
BLACK MESA PRESS
P.O. Box 583
Roswell, New Mexico 88202-0583
www.blackmesapress.com

All rights reserved. Except for the inclusion of brief quotations in a review, no part of this book may be reproduced in any form or by any electronic or mechanical means whatever, including photocopying, audio or video recording, or by any information storage and retrieval system without prior written permission of the author or publisher. For information, please write to the above address, or contact the author by telephone at 575-622-0855 or by e-mail at the address donaldrburleson @ yahoo.com

Cover art Copyright © Mollie L. Burleson
All rights reserved.

Library of Congress Control Number: 2002096048

ISBN-10:   0-9649580-5-8
ISBN-13:   978-0-9649580-5-0

Fourth printing July 2017

Printed in the United States by
Morris Publishing®
3212 East Highway 30
Kearney, NE 68847
1-800-650-7888

For Marilyn,
of course.

Acknowledgments

In trying to make sense out of the tragic circumstances of Marilyn Monroe's death, I am grateful to those earlier investigators who did much of the leg-work in uncovering basic facts– Anthony Summers, Robert Slatzer, Donald Wolfe, and others– because even though they made no connection with the field of UFO studies, they provided the basic framework of facts that made it possible for me to proceed with my own investigation.

I am profoundly grateful to the ever sharp-eyed and insightful Jane Shoemaker for first noticing the presence of an "imprint" on the Marilyn Monroe CIA memo and thus enabling me, after some image enhancement work, to make the critical "Schulgen connection."

My thanks go to all those colleagues, students, and friends at Eastern New Mexico University/Roswell and elsewhere who have encouraged me to pursue this project. I particularly want to thank all those who attended my Marilyn Monroe "going public" lecture on August 10, 2002 at the International UFO Museum and Research Center in Roswell. I am grateful to Dave Swink for coördinating this event, and to Pat Etherton for volunteering to videotape it for the Museum's archives.

Finally, my loving thanks to go my wonderful wife Mollie, for not only proofreading this book and doing the freehand sketch of Marilyn for the cover, but giving me, as always, her love and support throughout this work. Any errors here, however, are my own responsibility, and I trust they do not detract from my effort to set the record straight about the criminal conspiracy that brought about Marilyn's untimely death and its subsequent coverup.

It doesn't bring Marilyn back to say this, but I'll say it anyway– the coverup is over.

Unfortunately, the national disgrace that it represents never will be over.

Donald R. Burleson, Ph.D.
Roswell, New Mexico

Contents

1. Our Loss: This was Norma Jeane......................1

2. The Big Lie: Marilyn's "Suicide"...................... 8

3. Bad Company to Keep: The Kennedys...........19

4. August 4, 1962:
    A Night that will Live in Infamy.............. 31

5. The New Evidence:
    The Schulgen Connection......................53

6. The Crucial Hypothesis:
    Marilyn, JFK, and UFOs.........................70

7. Clincher: The Bolaños Interview...................80

8. The Press Conference that Never Was..........87

Recommended Reading....................................95

"Nay, lay thee down and roar;
For thou hast kill'd the sweetest innocent
That e'er did lift up eye."

Emilia, to Othello
after the murder of Desdemona

1.
Our Loss:
This was Norma Jeane

You never know what problems you'll end up working on when you become a UFO investigator. When I first entered the field of UFO studies years ago, I had no idea that I would find myself helping, in my own indirect but determined way, to investigate a murder. And I certainly never thought I would find myself helping, some decades after the fact, to investigate the murder of Marilyn Monroe.

On Saturday, August 4, 1962, when she died at approximately 10:45 p.m., Marilyn Monroe was the most famous woman in the world.

Today, nearly half a century after her tragic demise, Marilyn Monroe is *still* the most famous woman in the world.

It is no exaggeration whatever to say that she is an American icon, a legend, a culture hero, undeniably a part of our culture no less than Elvis or baseball. The memory of Marilyn Monroe will be with us always. She is not merely an integral part of what it is, culturally, to be American– in the uniqueness of her character, she is an integral part of what it is to be human. She was strong, she was frail; she had the capacity to be victor or victim. In short, she was and is a symbol of the human condition.

Marilyn wasn't perfect, certainly. She was sometimes petulant, sometimes possessed of unrealistic social ambitions, and– ultimately her downfall– sometimes naïve in her choice of companions and in her assessment of their actual feelings for her.

Over a hundred books have been written about Marilyn Monroe. A very few of these– notably Norman Mailer's *Marilyn* (1973), Anthony Summers' *Goddess: The Secret Lives of Marilyn Monroe* (1985), Robert F. Slatzer's *The Marilyn Files* (1992), and Donald H. Wolfe's *The Last Days of Marilyn Monroe* (1998)– actually manage to do a good job of getting under the glitter and the mythology to illumine a real and remarkable human being, as well as the real and appalling crime that was committed against her. The books mentioned are all undeniably excellent pieces of biography and investigative journalism, and I do not propose here to give the world yet another biography of Marilyn Monroe when others have done so with such success. My own present work is not a biography, but rather a kind of thanatography, an account of a death rather than a life, yet with a difference— I propose here to give new arguments to help explain *why* Marilyn died, a victim of murder, at the age of thirty-six. Since the reasons, as I claim, have to do with UFO-related government secrets, some people will no doubt scoff. Let them. The evidence, as we will see, speaks for itself. In any event, this is a book not so much about Marilyn's highly dynamic life as about the sinister circumstances of her death.

Nevertheless I feel compelled to say *something* about Marilyn's life, not to retrace old ground but rather to impart, for present purposes, a sense of the loss we all incurred when certain persons, for the sake of keeping very deep and dark government secrets covered up, ended Marilyn's life by lethal injection in the guest cottage of her home at 12305 Fifth Helena Drive in Brentwood, California. She was young, she was lovely, she was vibrant, and— suddenly— she was dead.

First, it is important to understand that the Marilyn Monroe known to the world of motion picture fans was largely the sort of construct that Hollywood has always been so clever at creating for their own inimitable moneymaking purposes. The "dumb blonde" image was wholly a movie star myth, and Marilyn in fact deeply resented it. But the Tinseltown camera capitalists knew the consumer psychology of ticket sales perfectly well. "See the beautiful, lithe young girl," their imagery whispered in the ears of hormonally active male moviegoers– "she's luscious and she's not too bright, so you could probably have her if you tried." Their appeal to the archetypal male fantasy world over the years would sell movie tickets by the millions, or so they figured.

Actually, what they never quite admitted to themselves, until it was too late, was that Marilyn's unique artistry as an actress went a long way toward explaining her popularity too. The moviegoing public always took Marilyn Monroe a lot more seriously than her producers and directors did. Nonetheless, long-lasting movie popularity requires creating a film persona, and the money movers created one. Their fascinating film goddess, who was always paid only a tiny fraction of what her equally-billed colleagues made, bought the studio moguls many a new swimming pool, many a European vacation.

Dumb blonde? Airhead? Not on your life. What can one say about a woman who loved the music of Béla Bartók? A woman who quoted freely from the novels of Thomas Wolfe and the poetry of Robert Browning? A woman who loved Shakespeare and wanted to play the part of Lady Macbeth someday? A woman who went out of her way to cultivate the acquaintance of the poet Carl Sandburg? A woman who sat down and read James Joyce's notoriously difficult *Ulysses*? I once read *Ulysses* too, but in a graduate course with a professor who guided her graduate students through the novel's labyrinthine complexities. Marilyn read it on her own, for pleasure. She was a voracious reader and a quick and avid learner. Although she never quite finished high school (she got married to Jim Dougherty when she was only sixteen), she made her learning a lifelong concern.

Her origins were humble and fraught with difficulties. Born in the charity ward of the General Hospital of Los Angeles on June 1, 1926 as Norma Jeane Mortensen, the Gemini girl who would be reborn as Marilyn Monroe had, as her earliest childhood recollection, the frightful memory of nearly being smothered in her bed by her insane grandmother Della Monroe, and indeed would herself live in the shadow of madness and deprivation, as her mother Gladys was in and out of mental hospitals and her father (presumably a man named Stan Gifford) was nowhere to be found. Norma Jeane spent her childhood alternately in an orphanage and in a series of foster homes, where she would be afflicted with stuttering and with chronic sleep disorders.

But she would also grow up to be stunningly beautiful, and this was to be both her blessing and her curse. Her blessing, because it was while working as a model that she was discovered by the motion picture industry, and acting would become the passion and the essence of her life. Yet beauty was her curse too, because men were always to find it difficult to see past her exquisite good looks and perceive the real, thinking, feeling woman beneath the physical goddess. Marilyn Monroe would find herself lonely, would experience four unsuccessful marriages (to Jim Dougherty, to Bob Slatzer, to Joe DiMaggio, and to Arthur Miller), would live in a constant and largely frustrated quest for true love. Many would fall in lust with her, but few would fall in love with her.

Lonely or not, Marilyn gave herself to the world of film with a dedication and a zest for perfection that many people have not wholly understood. She was sometimes resented by her colleagues on the sound stage, and undeniably she brought much of this upon herself. Often late to show up on the set when a movie was being made, she came across as inconsiderate to others. While her tardiness (she once quipped, "I've been on calendars, but never on *Time*) was sometimes due to severe sinusitis and other medical problems, it cannot be denied that she often had no good reason to keep everybody waiting, wasting both time and money.

On the other hand, when fellow actors thought her aloof or unfriendly on the set, they just didn't understand her attitude toward her art. Some actors are comfortable "dropping out of character" and chatting and telling jokes when the camera pauses, but Marilyn was not. She often kept to herself on a corner of the set, not because she was conceited or wanted to be unconvivial, but because she needed to keep her head squarely within the head of the character whom she was portraying. Acting was her art, and she wanted to get it right.

It seems fair to say that she indeed *did* get it right, throughout a remarkable if sadly foreshortened career that spanned from her first bit part in *The Shocking Miss Pilgrim* through such movies as *The Asphalt Jungle, All About Eve, How to Marry a Millionaire, Bus Stop, Gentlemen Prefer Blondes,* and *The Seven Year Itch,* all the way up to *The Misfits,* which she completed, and *Something's Got to Give,* which she never lived to complete.

She never lived to complete it, because she was murdered in her own home.

Murdered for the sake of keeping government secrets. It's a nasty story, but I'm going to tell it.

2.
The Big Lie: Marilyn's "Suicide"

Nearly half a century after her death, one still reads, from some commentators who speak either from ignorance or from some less than respectable agenda, that Marilyn Monroe committed suicide.

This myth, although easy to refute as we shall observe, is remarkably tenacious, and this is exceedingly unfortunate– because not only did Marilyn's tormentors murder her; they subjected her to character assassination as well. The thought that one has taken one's own life is one of the most tragic stigmata that can be imposed. Imagine that your wife or your sister or your mother has not only been murdered, but has also been "set up" after death to look like a suicide, in order to conceal the guilt of her killers. No more heinous crime against an innocent human being can readily be imagined. In Marilyn's case, it wasn't enough for them to murder her; they had to try to murder the quality of her memory as well.

For purposes of disproving the suicide myth, we have two avenues of approach: an examination of her apparent attitudes and feelings during the final days, the final hours, of her life; and an examination of her blood chemistry at the time of death.

One can argue, to some extent, about the psychology of attitudes and feelings. Not even all psychologists can agree on exactly what blend of mental states might most likely conduce to suicide. But one cannot argue with blood chemistry. Science is science, and we know much more about some things now (e.g. barbiturate poisoning) than was known in 1962 when Marilyn died.

Fortunately, Marilyn's toxicology report, compiled by Dr. A. J. Abernethy, remained intact over the years, filed away at the Los Angeles Hall of Records, and it is the toxicology report that tells the real story.

Marilyn's autopsy report was another matter. The coroner, Dr. Theodore Curphey, was basically a government-serving toady, evidently having readily been persuaded, by the shadow-figures in this whole sordid business, to coöperate in an orchestrated coverup. Curphey removed materials, or allowed the removal of materials, from Marilyn's file, to the point where a file originally consisting of 723 pages shrank to a comparatively meager 54 pages. At a time when, under such suspicious circumstances, he should have been ordering a coroner's inquest, he was pilfering files and lying to his employees to conceal– what? Clearly, the guilt of someone known to him, and probably someone pressuring him to do just that.

When the death certificate, marked "Probable suicide," crossed Coroner's Aide Lionel Grandison's desk to be signed, he was disturbed to see that after a history of pilferage (which he had himself observed) of the Marilyn Monroe file, the certificate arrived with no supporting paperwork at all. Dr. Grandison, who had always gravely doubted that there was sufficient reason to believe that Marilyn killed herself, complained to Dr. Curphey. The coroner simply told him, "Sign it, or something is going to happen." Grandison, who admitted to the press twenty years later in 1982 that he "agreed" only under duress, signed the certificate to avoid what would probably otherwise have been the ruin of his career. He was a young black man, fairly new to his profession, and I wouldn't be at all surprised if, given the social climate of the times, his ethnicity played a part in the pressures brought to bear upon him to sign a document that he strongly suspected to be fraudulent (which indeed it was).

Dr. Curphey, the Los Angeles County Coroner, was definitely a manipulator of people for his own purposes, or (more likely) for the purposes of people whose agendas he was carrying out. For example, it is not without significance that he assigned Marilyn's autopsy to Dr. Thomas Noguchi, who at the time was *Deputy* Medical Examiner for Los Angeles County and therefore was, relatively speaking, an underling. This way Curphey (who uncharacteristically stuck around for *this* autopsy instead of just leaving it to others) was able to call all the shots, directing the whole procedure along the lines he wanted to see it follow. His suppression of evidence, with regard to the rifled Marilyn Monroe files, speaks volumes about his inclination toward manipulation and fraud.

But in any case the toxicology report turns out to be the decisively telling document. According to Dr. Abernethy's analysis of the blood sample taken and passed along by Dr. Noguchi, Marilyn's blood contained 4.5 milligrams per cent pentobarbital and 8.0 milligrams per cent chloral hydrate. That is, in terms of density of toxins in the bloodstream, Marilyn had 4.5 milligrams of pentobarbital per 100 milliliters of blood volume, and 8.0 milligrams of chloral hydrate per 100 milliliters of blood volume. As any toxicologist can affirm, this is a deadly combination, and in the toxic density described it would have been enough to kill a whole roomful of people.

Now, the popular and deliberately propagated misconception is that Marilyn died by overdosing on pills, Nembutal being the barbiturate that would have been responsible in particular. (The night that Marilyn died, her psychiatrist Dr. Ralph Greenson made a big show of pointing out pill bottles to the police at Marilyn's house.) But there are definite problems with the "pill overdose" hypothesis.

For one thing, computer analyses of many thousands of cases of acute barbiturate poisoning have been carried out during the years since Marilyn's death, and it is known now that in all cases where someone took as many as a dozen Nembutal capsules, their digestive tract always contained capsule residue, barbiturate concentrations, or distinctive refractive crystal traces. (Crystalline substances found in the stomach or intestines generally have a "refractive index" by which they can be identified.) To reach Marilyn's level of blood toxicity, one would have to ingest upwards of fifty capsules (Nembutal and chloral hydrate combined), at the very least; yet Marilyn's digestive tract was found to contain only 20 cc's of clear fluid, and absolutely *no* refractile crystals, capsule residue, or barbiturate concentrations whatever.

When journalists Peter Harry Brown and Patte B. Barham (as described in their book *Marilyn: The Last Take*) spoke with Abbott Laboratories, where Nembutal capsules are manufactured, a spokesperson told them that it was "just not possible" for Marilyn to reach the described level of blood toxicity by ingesting capsules, as the spokesperson estimated it would require

Marilyn's taking from seventy-five to ninety capsules (and death would ensue long before she finished doing it). Also, Abbott Labs chemists told Marilyn's friend Bob Slatzer, "It might have taken far more than ninety!" And these people ought to know– they *make* the pills!

Marilyn, by the way, according to her friend Bob Slatzer, had trouble even swallowing an aspirin without choking on it, unless she had a big glass of water. There was no water glass in the bedroom where the police found her body, and in fact the water had been turned off in the bathroom that adjoined that bedroom, due to ongoing repairs. The "closed bedroom suicide" scenario makes no sense in a room in which there is no access to water and no initial evidence that any water was present.

Here's the best way of looking at what's wrong with the "pill overdose" theory. Suppose you decide to try to do to your own blood chemistry what had been done to Marilyn's, and insisted on doing it by ingestion of pills. So you sit down and surround yourself with ample supplies of barbiturates and chloral hydrate ("mickey finn") tablets, together with a couple of pitchers of water, with a view to raising your blood toxicity to 4.5 milligrams per cent pentobarbital and 8.0 milligrams per cent chloral hydrate. You start gobbling pills. A small fraction of the way through this grim process, you would die. Your heart would stop, the circulation of your blood would stop, the absorption of materials from your digestive tract into your bloodstream would abruptly and completely cease. Consequently a couple of things would happen: (1) Your blood toxicity would fall a *long* way short of the levels you were aiming at; and (2) your stomach or intestines or both would contain easily detectable quantities of residue from the swallowed but unabsorbed drugs.

The same objections apply to the "infusion by enema" theory sometimes proposed. It is simply not possible to load oneself up with enough enema-infused barbiturates and choral hydrate concentrations to raise one's blood toxin density as high as that which was found in Marilyn's blood sample. The victim would be dead long before the blood chemistry assumed those proportions.

The *only* way to produce that kind of blood chemistry is by *direct needle injection*. And Marilyn sure as hell didn't do that to herself. According to close friends, she neither owned a hypodermic needle nor knew how to use one.

Reportedly, Dr. Noguchi found no needle marks during the autopsy. However, Dr. Hyman Engleberg, Marilyn's internist, had given her routine medical injections only a few days before her death (he presented a bill for them to her estate), and Dr. Noguchi didn't find those needle marks either. As is well known, such marks are easily obscured by lividity (the tendency of noncirculating blood to pool up, by gravity, at low points in the body)– and indeed Marilyn's body, found face-down, exhibited lividity on her front side. The evidence is decisive, from her blood chemistry. Marilyn was killed by lethal injection. As it could scarcely have been an accident on anyone's part (the toxicity in her blood was many times the density of any ordinary sedative dosage), this whole pattern of evidence clearly suggests premeditated homicide.

An examination of her evident state of mind, as indicated by her circumstances and by observations of her friends (her *real* friends), will certainly go a long way toward discrediting the suicide notion as well. The whole picture of Marilyn's outlook in early August of 1962 is one that makes it exceedingly unlikely– indeed virtually inconceivable– that she might have been thinking of taking her own life.

In the summer of 1962 there were those of course who tried their hardest to initiate and perpetuate a suicidal-depression myth. For years actor Peter Lawford, for example, would tell everyone who would listen that Marilyn was suicidally despondent over having been fired by the management of Twentieth Century Fox, who also discontinued the movie that Marilyn was supposed to be making with them, *Something's Got to Give*. Their complaint was that Marilyn had missed far too many days on the set.

But Lawford knew perfectly well that this account was misleading; he did his best to spread this convenient "despondency" notion around in keeping with his own not inconsiderable part in the ongoing coverup of Marilyn's murder. Marilyn had indeed been fired by Fox, in mid-June 1962, but she had been reinstated only a week and a half later (apparently at the instigation, at least in part, of Robert Kennedy, who held great influence over the board at Fox and was essentially manipulating Marilyn's career, in effect holding her career hostage for his own purposes)– in fact, she was not only reinstated, but rehired at five times her previous contractual salary. She had been making *Something's Got to Give* for $100,000 but was offered $500,000 in the new negotiation; also Fox had offered her another $500,000 to take a part in another planned film to be called *What a Way to Go*. There were also plans for a new musical version of *A Tree Grows in Brooklyn*, in which both Frank Sinatra and Marilyn Monroe were to have starring roles. Not only that, but Marilyn had found a new and powerful ally in Darryl F. Zanuch, who after a long absence had regained control of Twentieth Century Fox. Peter Lawford knew all this but kept right on telling the big lie about Marilyn's "depression."

    The truth is that Marilyn was ecstatic over her burgeoning career prospects, and why shouldn't she have been, with a million-dollar contract sitting on her attorney Mickey Rudin's desk, just waiting for her signature? Actress Jeanne Carmen, her close friend and former neighbor, remarked that in those first few days of August 1962 she had never seen Marilyn so happy, so upbeat, so glad to be alive, so thoroughly looking forward to the future. At the time of her death, Marilyn's house was cluttered with at least twenty movie scripts that she was reading, and telegrams had arrived offering her all sorts of movie deals. She was very much in demand, and she loved the idea of being so.

If there was any negative emotionality invading Marilyn's peace of mind during those last few days, it was *anger*. She was angry about a number of things. First of all, President John F. Kennedy and United States Attorney General Robert F. Kennedy, both of whom had had romantic entanglements with her, had suddenly distanced themselves from Marilyn, refusing her phone calls, cutting her off abruptly and without explanation. She was angry with her press agent Pat Newcomb; Marilyn on the day of her death had had an argument with her. (The reasons for this are uncertain, but considering the behavior of the Kennedy brothers, Marilyn's displeasure with Newcomb probably had a lot to do with the latter's loyalties to the Kennedy family.)

Marilyn was angry with her housekeeper Eunice Murray, whom she had come to distrust, and in fact she fired her on that last day, August 4th. Marilyn was fed up with her psychiatrist Dr. Ralph Greenson and had finally resolved to rid herself of him as well. In Marilyn's heyday it was standard practice for actors to have psychiatrists or analysts, purportedly in order to come to "know themselves" and thus presumably be better equipped emotionally to play parts in movies. Having an analyst was practically a professional status symbol in Hollywood, and Marilyn was essentially just following this pattern. (She had been referred to Greenson by her New York analyst Marianne Kris, who was a personal friend of Sigmund Freud.) But Marilyn had become weary of playing the game, and had pretty much decided she didn't need Greenson any more.

Clearly she was shucking off, one by one, the negative influences in her life so that nothing would cloud the bright future that her new film prospects were promising her. She was doing this "housecleaning" in fits of anger, but as any psychologist can tell you, anger is not an emotion that of itself readily tends to suicide. Depression or despondency, yes. Anger, no. Anger typically makes one want to stick around and impose the effects of one's anger on others. Anger makes one defiant and confrontational. It does not make one want to end one's own life.

Marilyn Monroe did not commit suicide. The notion that she did is a longstanding lie perpetuated most strongly by those who had the most powerful motive for doing so– to cover up their own guilt, or the guilt of others close to them, with regard to culpable involvement in Marilyn's untimely and unnecessary death.

3.
Bad Company to Keep: the Kennedys

To say that John F. Kennedy was a "womanizer" would scarcely capture the spirit of the thing. The expression "love 'em and leave 'em" acquires a whole new level of meaning when it applies to JFK. Given that the man used to boast to his friends that he had had intimate relations with over 1,300 different women, one easily accepts the remark, once made of JFK, that to him another woman was pretty much like just another cup of coffee. His father Joe Kennedy, himself an able maker of the romantic rounds (he had a notorious affair with Gloria Swanson, and heaven knows whom else), is said once to have advised all his boys, "Get laid every chance you get." JFK, for one, certainly seems to have taken this touching paternal advice to heart.

Apparently well-nigh irresistible to women (at least until they found out what he was really like), the boy who would be President of the United States no doubt began his romantic conquests early in life, and the details of many of his earliest escapades will never be known. An incident occurred in 1941, however, that turns out to have significant implications.

In that year, only a few months before Pearl Harbor and the entrance of the United States into World War II, Jack Kennedy, at the age of 24 and with the help of his father's always powerful influence, became commissioned as an ensign in the Naval Reserve and was assigned to the Office of Naval Intelligence in Washington, where he worked on a daily basis with classified information. In D.C. he met an attractive young Danish journalist named Inga Arvad, who wrote a sort of gossip column for the *Washington Times-Herald*. A torrid love affair ensued, and for the first time but hardly the last, Jack Kennedy's social life painted him as a possible security risk in the eyes of J. Edgar Hoover, director of the FBI.

The problem was that FBI operatives suspected Inga Arvad of being a Nazi spy, ensconced in her post in the nation's capital for the purpose of rooting out secret information. It would eventually turn out that these suspicions were probably untrue, but Inga's onetime association with such Nazi VIPs as Himmler, Goebbels, and even Adolf Hitler himself didn't do her cause any good in the estimation of the FBI. (Hitler regarded her as conforming nicely to his halfwit notion of the ideal "blonde Aryan" super-race.) Consequently

Justice Department operatives had her, and then JFK, under surveillance.

But for Joe Kennedy's probable intercession, the Navy might well have had Jack discharged altogether, but as it was, they reassigned him to a relatively innocuous desk job in Charleston, South Carolina. Inga, however, evidently too taken with the young ensign's charms to be so easily daunted, followed him to his new place of duty, and the affair continued.

At this point the FBI was even more disturbed that the move from D.C. to Charleston hadn't ended things between Jack and Inga (Jack still knew many things that were highly classified, after all), and J. Edgar Hoover used his own influence to have JFK transferred again, this time to duty in the South Pacific. No doubt Hoover thought he had put the young upstart Kennedy out of the picture for good, but (from Hoover's point of view) the plan backfired in the long run, in that when JFK came back as a war hero, his prospects for a successful political career were much enhanced. Now John Kennedy would continue to be a thorn in Hoover's side for many years to come.

For present purposes, the significance of the Inga Arvad episode is that in an eerie way it seems to have foreshadowed the whole Marilyn Monroe problem. In carrying on an extended affair with Inga, even when it had become very clear that his actions were making him a security risk because of the sensitive nature of his (original) job with the Navy, JFK set a clear pattern of active priorities– and the pattern was that at least at times, his hormonal needs overshadowed his sense of official propriety, even his sense of the exigencies of national security. Apparently, for JFK, the old wartime maxim "Loose lips sink ships" didn't always penetrate into the bedroom. Not that (so far as is known) he ever actually passed classified information along to Inga, or not that she necessarily wanted him to, but it's certainly easy to see why the FBI was so concerned at the time.

After the war, when JFK's political career was beginning, his romantic fancy soon turned to thoughts of movie stars. After winning the 1946 primary in Boston that would lead to his gaining a seat in the United States Senate, he went to Hollywood for a vacation, and one can only gather that he enjoyed it supremely. The list of motion picture lady luminaries who fell under the sway of that charming smile is spectacularly impressive (starting with Gene Tierney and Peggy Cummins), and indeed over the years JFK probably *earned* that boast to his friends that he had bedded over 1,300 women, many of them well known on the silver screen.

Accounts differ as to exactly when his ongoing affair with Marilyn Monroe started. He is said possibly to have met her as early as 1951 at a party given by Marilyn's agent Charlie Feldman. JFK can scarcely be blamed for being attracted to her; *everyone* was attracted to her, and not merely because of her physical beauty. (As Robert Slatzer has said, she possessed a kind of primal magnetism that riveted everyone's attention upon her when she walked into a room. There was something magical about her, as anyone who ever met her can attest.)

    Certainly by the time Marilyn was married to Joe DiMaggio in 1954 Kennedy was starting to eye her predatorily, much to the indignation of an understandably jealous Joe. There is plentiful evidence that during the late 1950s JFK and Marilyn were an "item." He was Senator John Kennedy then, and in 1960 when he ran for President, Marilyn was an active supporter. Clearly, she had dreams of one day being First Lady. Unlike JFK's other female conquests, Marilyn seems to have had the power to keep him coming back to her time after time. She was decidedly not a one-night stand to him, but there was never any chance that he was going to marry her. In the end JFK never really cared for his women. Marilyn's tragic flaw, the setup for her ultimate undoing, was being so naïve as to think that he did care for her.

    Interestingly enough, in July 1962 just after he had broken things off with Marilyn, and just weeks before her death, Jack Kennedy had another affair that possibly carried implications for national security, and for the relation between JFK's personal life and his regard for the responsibilities of office. It seems he fell in with an artist named Mary Pinchot Meyer, and the name of the game this time was not only sex but drugs. Mary, on at least one of her visits to the White House, enticed JFK to smoke some marijuana with her, and on another occasion is supposed to have accompanied him on an LSD trip as well.

While drug experiments may be of relatively little consequence for many people, they clearly constitute a more dangerous game for the person holding arguably the most important, sensitive, and powerful political office on the planet. Jack Kennedy himself is said once to have commented, to Mary upon her offering him yet another joint to smoke, "Suppose the Russians drop a bomb." Whether he was kidding or not we don't know, but this remark in any case shows that it occurred even to JFK to wonder at times about the propriety of his recreational activities.

Intriguingly, his wayward lady friend Mary Pinchot Meyer was murdered in Georgetown in October 1964. Robert Kennedy's biographer C. David Heymann reports in his book *RFK: A Candid Biography of Robert F. Kennedy* that "[e]vidence in the case suggests that Mary was the shooting victim of either FBI or CIA agents who might have believed that in the course of her relationship with the president, he could have divulged important state secrets."

Thus the case of Marilyn Monroe was neither the first nor the last time John Kennedy was at least suspected of passing along sensitive information, or being in the position to do so, to unauthorized persons. When the FBI and the CIA became alarmed that precisely that kind of thing might have been happening with Marilyn, the situation fit the pattern that permeated JFK's whole career, lending all the more plausibility to the notion that JFK had indeed become a security risk in his relationship with Marilyn. (The difference was, in Marilyn's case we have reason to think that the state secrets divulged were UFO-related. But the other cases serve to illustrate that JFK was habitually careless about classified information.)

Of course Jack wasn't the only Kennedy to become entangled with Marilyn. There was also Robert Francis Kennedy.

JFK astonished even some political insiders when, upon his being elected President, he gave in to the urging of Joe Kennedy and appointed little brother Bobby as Attorney General of the United States. Bobby had never even practiced law and had virtually no qualifications to be Attorney General, though he was well educated and certainly ambitious. Bobby would pursue the duties of his new office with zeal, tangling in many a colorful confrontation with Jimmy Hoffa and other luminaries of organized crime. (This is of course deliciously ironic, as the Chicago mob manipulated elections to help put JFK in the Oval Office and thus, indirectly, to help make Bobby the Attorney General.)

While some commentators have suggested that

Bobby may have met Marilyn Monroe earlier, it is likely he didn't actually meet her until a party in February 1962 at Peter Lawford's famous beach house. Bobby was clearly taken with her (and again, who could blame him for that?)– what's more, the attraction seems to have been mutual, even though Marilyn's fascination with JFK continued.

Bobby, after all, was something of a womanizer himself, though not to the extent that his brother JFK was. (Bobby's own affairs included Lee Remick, Jayne Mansfield, and even Mary Jo Kopechne of *Teddy* Kennedy fame at Chappaquiddick. As Alice remarked, things get curiouser and curiouser.) JFK, let's face it, was something of a jerk, in that he viewed his countless women *only* as conquests and made very little effort to try to conceal his dalliances. Bobby was a jerk too, big time, but he was a more *careful* jerk, in that he did make at least some effort to be discreet about his extramarital affairs.

Indeed when the relationship between JFK and Marilyn Monroe was fairly well known, the relationship between RFK and Marilyn was a rather better-kept secret. Throughout the early months of 1962 the classic love triangle existed, with JFK having the upper hand in Marilyn's eyes at first, though she was intrigued with Bobby as well, often following him around and jotting down things that he said. The Peter Lawford beach house in Santa Monica, not far from Marilyn's house in

Brentwood, had long since become the prime party place and playhouse for the Kennedys, and both JFK and RFK enjoyed flings with Marilyn there. The place was bugged by organized crime figures (notably, as legend has it, Jimmy Hoffa) for the purposes of obtaining blackmail material on the Kennedys, particularly on Bobby as Attorney General, since it was he who was on their (organized crime's) case, as it were. Marilyn would come to tire of this "party palace" scenario, complaining to friends that Peter Lawford and the Kennedys sometimes had her over in the company of invited prostitutes. These guys sent out for whores the way most of us might send out for pizza, and Marilyn mightily resented being, for all appearances, associated in the Kennedy minds with prostitutes. But her affairs with both Kennedy brothers continued.

Things came to something of a crisis when Marilyn, largely at the instigation of "brother-in-Lawford," came to Madison Square Garden on May 19, 1962 (AWOL from her duties on the set of the movie-in-progress *Something's Got to Give*) and sang her notoriously sexy "happy birthday" to JFK in front of a large and distinguished crowd. Bobby Kennedy went to her dressing room beforehand and apparently tried to discourage her from going on; hairdresser Mickey Song could hear them through the closed door, arguing, and after Bobby left, Song found Marilyn with her hair disheveled and had to get her ready all over again.

As anyone who has seen the film of Marilyn's "happy birthday" performance can attest (she wore a dress that was as next-to-nothing as one could get away with in front of cameras), her serenade to JFK was pretty much an act of seduction. Jackie Kennedy apparently expected something of the sort; upon hearing that the event was planned, she arranged to be out of town, opting to go horseback riding in Virginia rather than attend her own husband's birthday party.

After the party the Kennedys and select company, including Marilyn (although she wasn't feeling at all well), gathered at film mogul Arthur Krim's New York penthouse for drinks. To Ethel Kennedy's great annoyance, Bobby danced repeatedly with Marilyn. Also Marilyn and Bobby and Jack gathered later in a corner for what looked like an earnest conversation. Photographs were taken, but government officials showed up the next morning at the photo lab at *Time* Magazine and confiscated the photos and negatives. (One photo survived.)

After the Krim party, Marilyn accompanied JFK to his hotel suite nearby and *really* wished him a happy birthday. It was the last time they ever saw each other. Seventy-seven days later, Marilyn would be dead.

A few days after the birthday bash, FBI chief J. Edgar Hoover had a conference with Jack Kennedy. It appears that Hoover laid the law down to JFK about the President's having become a security risk due to his intimate association with Marilyn Monroe, who was known to be keeping company with a number of left-wing people (including her psychiatrist Ralph Greenson). Hoover seems to have prevailed, because JFK immediately had Marilyn's private line to the White House disconnected. According to those close to the Kennedy brothers, JFK also at this time essentially asked Bobby to entertain Marilyn and get him off his (JFK's) back.

This was a job that Bobby didn't in the least mind taking on, though he might have minded, if he had known the troubles that lay ahead.

Even with Bobby's increased attention to her, Marilyn was disturbed to learn, with increasing clarity during the last few weeks of her life, that JFK really was determined to have nothing more to do with her. Bobby, meanwhile, may even have offered at some point to divorce Ethel and marry Marilyn; as unlikely as this promise was to be kept, surveillance tapes from the Lawford and Monroe houses did make it sound as if Bobby had made rash promises which Marilyn became all too insistent upon holding him to.

In the end, Marilyn felt rejected by *both* Kennedy brothers, and with good reason. Like JFK, Bobby at length made himself inaccessible to Marilyn by phone. The Kennedys had dropped her, distanced themselves from her. She was furious with them, and during the final two or three days of her life she began telling close friends that she might just hold a news conference and "tell all."

That expressed intention, as it turns out, was her death warrant. If she had just gone ahead and done it– if she had just *called* a press conference– everything would have been different.

Everything.

But in an age of electronic surveillance Marilyn made the mistake of talking about the planned news conference first.

And she never lived to carry it out.

Someone highly placed in government couldn't afford to let her carry it out.

4.
August 4, 1962 : A Night that will Live in Infamy

One of the most difficult problems that an investigator can encounter is the task of establishing a time-line, a clear and disentangled sequence of events, in a situation in which the real nature of the occurrences has been deliberately obscured, distorted, covered up.

This predicament is one that is familiar to many UFO investigators, and particularly familiar to anyone who has worked (as I have) on the "Roswell time-line" problem. (Puzzlements abound in the Roswell case. When did the Army really retrieve the UFO wreckage? What did various people know about the crash at various times?) The problem of sorting out the sequentiality of events on the night of Marilyn Monroe's death is in many ways eerily similar.

Much of what one reads about the hours just

before and after Marilyn's death is confusing and inconsistent, precisely because key figures in the narrative have told contradictory stories, fabrications deliberately designed to conceal the truth. Capable independent investigations have been carried out, however, notably including the work of Bob Slatzer, Anthony Summers, and Donald Wolfe, and this work, when one follows it carefully and thinks it through, makes it possible to separate distortion from reality, fabrication from truth, especially when one considers this investigative work in the light of what (I will argue) the real *reasons* were for Marilyn's murder, and especially when one eliminates specious alternative accounts by examining the weakness of their logic.

One of the primary participants in this bizarre drama was Marilyn's housekeeper Eunice Murray, whose son-in-law Norman Jeffries also worked around the place as a handyman. Eunice Murray was a longtime acquaintance of Dr. Ralph Greenson, Marilyn's psychiatrist, who seems to have pushed Eunice upon Marilyn in early 1962 for the purpose of keeping an eye on the film goddess in her own newly purchased house. Eunice had apparently had some experience in psychiatric nursing.

In the late afternoon of that fateful Saturday, August 4, 1962, Marilyn received a visit from "the general" (as she had dubbed him in happier times) Robert Kennedy and his brother-in-law Peter Lawford.

Eunice Murray and Norman Jeffries were there when they arrived, and were told in firm terms that they should leave the house and go out and do some shopping, as the visitors wanted to speak to Marilyn alone. (Sometimes the Kennedy arrogance knew no bounds.) Eunice and her son-in-law did as they were told. (For years afterward, Peter Lawford would claim that Bobby wasn't even in Los Angeles that day. Plainly, he was lying to protect his brother-in-law. Also, Eunice Murray would not until 1985 admit that Bobby Kennedy had been present at Marilyn's house that Saturday.)

Audio surveillance in place in the house at the time reveals that Bobby Kennedy and Marilyn had a violent argument that afternoon. Marilyn complained to Bobby that he had promised to divorce Ethel and marry her but had broken his promise. She complained that for the Kennedy brothers she seemed to be something to be just "passed around like a piece of meat." The argument grew more strident, and it became clear that Bobby was looking for something, as he kept screaming, "Where is it? Where the fuck is it?" and things to the effect, "My family must have it," and "We'll make any arrangements you want," and "We'll pay you for it." In retrospect, it's obvious that Bobby was looking for Marilyn's diary. (Some early investigators speculated that Bobby was looking for the "bug" in Marilyn's house, but it scarcely would have made sense for him to say that his family would "pay for" that.)

Marilyn had been a diary-keeper all her life, and her most recent one was a little red book in which she was known to have scribbled, among other things, notes on things she and Bobby Kennedy had talked about, including political matters and foreign affairs. Jeanne Carmen has recalled seeing Bobby grab up Marilyn's red diary in her living room one day and hurl it across the room, shouting "Get rid of this!"

Obviously the diary was a matter of grave concern to Bobby Kennedy. Later we will see very revealing references to the diary in a CIA document; Bobby wasn't the only one concerned about it. The big question was: what sensitive governmental matters might Marilyn have jotted down? People who saw the diary (e.g. Robert Slatzer) said that it contained, at the least, references to the Kennedys, Jimmy Hoffa, and Fidel Castro; the question is, though— what were Bobby and other people afraid it *might* contain?

Whatever it was, Bobby's verbal demands for the diary grew ever more desperate-sounding on the surveillance tapes, until he was shrieking in a high-pitched and hysterical way that made his voice hard to recognize, while Peter Lawford could be heard urging him to calm down. From the sound of things, Bobby slapped Marilyn around a bit, before she finally ordered both of them the hell out of her house and slammed the door. It is quite clear that Bobby Kennedy and Peter Lawford had visited Marilyn that afternoon in hopes of placating her, keeping her quiet, getting her to coöperate and hand over the now famous diary. It was already known at this point, from various wiretaps, that Marilyn was threatening to hold a press conference that Monday morning, August 6th, and *that idea* had Bobby plenty worried. Even so, he must have figured he could get her to behave. But instead of the compliant pushover he and Lawford had hoped to find at 12305 Fifth Helena Drive, they encountered a stubborn, fiery-tempered blonde hellion who had no inclination whatever to yield to Bobby Kennedy's demands.

When Eunice Murray and Norman Jeffries returned to the house after their enforced shopping trip, they found Marilyn in a very upset and angry state. Note— not despondent, not moping. She was *angry*, so angry that her hands were shaking with rage. She would no doubt gladly have strangled Bobby at that moment if she could have gotten her hands on him. Eunice called Dr. Greenson, who came over and spent a couple of hours getting Marilyn calmed down. Greenson asked Eunice to stay at Marilyn's house overnight, even though Marilyn had fired her earlier in the day. Eunice in turn asked Norman Jeffries to stay over too.

No doubt the whole thing would essentially have ended right there, that afternoon, if Marilyn had been meek and coöperative, and if she had just said, "Okay, Bobby, here's my diary, and I promise to leave you and

Jack alone and not hold any press conferences and not make any trouble." But the way things ended up, Bobby knew quite well that his business with Marilyn was unresolved. He would be coming back to her house on what turned out to be the night of her death.

But first, let's return to Eunice Murray, and skip ahead to her (as well as others') account of the night's events, to see how fabrication supplanted truth, and how Bobby Kennedy was involved.

On Dr. Greenson's advice, Marilyn went to bed early that night, having slept poorly the night before. She took one of the telephones into the bedroom with her, and spent the evening talking on the phone to various people, as was her custom. Eunice's *first* story to the police was that she saw light under Marilyn's bedroom door shortly after midnight and became alarmed. This couldn't have been true, because (as Robert Slatzer pointed out a few days later) there was a new carpet in the hall, and the nap of the carpet was so high that it was difficult to open the bedroom door; no light could possibly have shone through from the bedroom into the hall.

Anyway, Eunice would shortly change her story, saying that she didn't get alarmed about Marilyn until around 3:30 in the morning. Also, Eunice changed her account with regard to the reason for being alarmed, saying this time that she got worried upon seeing the phone cord still under Marilyn's bedroom door. This doesn't make any sense, though, because Marilyn commonly kept the phone with her at night, and the sight of the phone cord could hardly have been anything so unusual as to be any cause for alarm.

Marilyn's internist, Dr. Hyman Engleberg, originally said that he declared Marilyn dead at 12:30 a.m. Later he changed his story and said that he declared her dead at 3:50 a.m. How a physician could make such a "mistake" is hard to understand, unless he were being coached to adjust his story, which indeed all the participants appear to have been led to do.

Marilyn's publicist Pat Newcomb told interviewers that attorney Mickey Rudin (who, by the way, was Dr. Greenson's brother-in-law) called her around 4:00 a.m. to tell her that Marilyn was dead. This was a lie, as we know that Pat Newcomb knew about Marilyn's death before 11:00 p.m. that Saturday, and in fact came to the house before that time, with Peter Lawford. (Norman Jeffries saw them arrive together.)

The simple fact is that the participants in this drama adjusted their accounts to make it appear *that Marilyn's death occurred later than it really did*. It was known, after all, that Attorney General Robert F. Kennedy was at Marilyn's house both in the late afternoon and on the evening of August 4th. If Marilyn died close to the time when Bobby was last present at her house, then there would clearly be a problem for Bobby. But if Marilyn didn't die until Bobby had been gone for hours, then the problem would pretty well vanish. The synoptic picture is one of collaboration, conspiracy if you will, on everyone's part to see to it that Bobby's reputation was protected.

But the details don't add up. Fortunately for those of us who have a regard for the truth, logic works much better for truth-tellers than for liars. (It is an inherent weakness of coverups that they are typically done somewhat in haste, leaving it possible for later investigators to unravel all the poor logic at our leisure.)

For one thing, it's easy to prove not only that Marilyn was dead before 11:00 p.m., but that a number of people knew it.

On that Saturday night, Henry Mancini and his band played a concert at the Hollywood Bowl. Arthur Jacobs (head of the publicity agency for which Marilyn's publicist Pat Newcomb worked) had gone to the concert, taking his fiancée Natalie Trundy, the future Natalie Jacobs; it was Natalie's birthday. After Arthur Jacobs' death, his widow Natalie told interviewers that shortly before the end of the Mancini concert that night, a staff member came to Arthur and Natalie's box with a message from Pat Newcomb: Marilyn had suffered a lethal overdose of drugs.

Natalie recalled that Arthur left immediately, just before the concert was over, and that she didn't hear from him for a couple of days. (And when he next spoke with her, of his part in the activities at Marilyn's house, he only cryptically remarked to her, "I had to fudge the whole thing.") He must have received the message at the concert before 11:00 p.m., since there was a city ordinance in Los Angeles requiring the Hollywood Bowl to conclude its concerts by that hour, due to the proximity of the Bowl to residential streets.

Therefore Marilyn was dead before 11:00 p.m., and Eunice Murray, Ralph Greenson, and Hyman Engleberg were less than truthful when they claimed that her death occurred well after midnight. Engleberg was on even more dubious ground when he implied that her death occurred sometime after 3:00 a.m. (When Marilyn's body was placed on the gurney around 5:30 a.m., *rigor mortis* was already well advanced. It varies, but it usually takes five or six hours to set in to that extent, so death could not conceivably have occurred as late as Engleberg claimed.)

According to witness accounts, Arthur Jacobs, going to 12305 Fifth Helena Drive after leaving the Mancini concert, played a considerable part in the coverup operations that occurred between 11:00 p.m. and 4:25 a.m. when the police were finally called. Marilyn's house was rearranged, her body was moved from the guest cottage (where she died) to her bedroom (where great effort was expended to make it *look* as if she died there), papers were removed, and witnesses were coached into rethinking their stories to conceal the real time of Marilyn's death– approximately 10:45 p.m.

Saturday, *not* the wee hours of Sunday morning.

The true story has come to us from Norman Jeffries, Eunice's son-in-law and Marilyn's handyman. Interviewed in 1992 during his terminal illness, thirty years after the inception of the coverup, he revealed that he was on the scene during the entire nighttime episode (except for about half an hour when he was ordered to leave the house, and even then he was nearby) and saw and heard a sequence of events that other witnesses reported only partially and inaccurately. (Jeffries, after all, had no reason to lie at this point. The others all most decidedly *did* have reasons to lie, whether to conceal their own complicity and guilt, or to acquiesce in the coverup due to having been pressured, even threatened, by the powerful people who were ultimately responsible.)

Here, as well as the testimony of reliable witnesses has made it possible to tell, are the events of that awful night.

When Marilyn took the telephone to bed with her shortly after Dr. Greenson left her, urging her to get a good night's sleep, she spoke with a number of close friends by phone, and their recollections of these conversations suggest that she was in good spirits, though still angry about her row with Bobby Kennedy.

She called Peter Lawford around 7:30 p.m., and according to Lawford's dinner guests he just came back to the table and remarked nonchalantly that she had called. Lawford would later tell an unlikely story to the effect that Marilyn had called and said, "Say goodbye to the President." This was an attempt, afterward, to make it look as if Marilyn had been suicidally despondent. But according to Lawford's guests Joe and Dolores Naar, who were present until around 10:00 p.m., he gave no indication that anything unusual was going on, or that he was worried about Marilyn. Likely as not, considering the afternoon's events, Marilyn had some choice things to say to Lawford on the phone about his hysterical and tyrannical brother-in-law Bobby. (Lawford is said to have spoken later, around 10:30 p.m., to a distraught-sounding Marilyn whose voice faded away. Overall, though, Lawford's statements at various times were so inconsistent, disingenuous, and evasive that one can hardly derive anything informative from them.)

Sometime around 8:00 p.m., Marilyn spoke with Joe DiMaggio, Jr., who called her to chat about a girlfriend. According to Joe Jr., Marilyn sounded very normal and upbeat in mood.

Around 8:30 Marilyn spoke to her hairdresser Sidney Guilaroff. They talked about Marilyn's falling out with Bobby Kennedy, and planned on meeting the next day to discuss it some more. This is scarcely the sort of thing Marilyn would have said to a close associate if she had been planning to kill herself. Interestingly, she also commented to Guilaroff that she knew a lot of secrets derived from the Kennedy brothers. Guilaroff asked her what kind of secrets, and she only replied, enigmatically, "Dangerous ones." One has to wonder: dangerous to whom? Marilyn didn't elaborate.

She called her friend Jeanne Carmen around 9:00 and asked her to come over, but Jeanne begged off. She later said that Marilyn sounded "nervous and afraid," and that when the phone rang again later in the evening, she suspected it was Marilyn again but didn't answer this time. She would always regret it, though it seems unlikely that the outcome would have been any different if she had answered the second call, assuming it was from Marilyn.

A little after 9:00, Marilyn's old friend Henry Rosenfeld called her from New York, and they talked about a theater party Marilyn was planning for early September in D.C. near the time of the opening of the new Irving Berlin musical *Mr. President*, for which Rosenfeld was to be her escort. Again, these kinds of plans scarcely sound like the ruminations of a mind contemplating suicide.

Sometime just before 10:00 Marilyn received a call from her new romantic interest José Bolaños, the Mexican screenwriter and movie director she had met south of the border in February; he had been her escort to the Golden Globe Awards in March. Bolaños, who was calling from a nearby restaurant, later said that Marilyn, that night on the phone, told him "something shocking– something that will one day shock the whole world." (As will be seen, this remark is of tremendous importance.) Bolaños also said that Marilyn, rather than hanging up, just set the phone down, apparently going to check on what sounded like some sort of commotion at her front door. She never came back to the phone.

We know of these last telephone conversations of Marilyn's due to the testimony of those persons she spoke with, but we know the rest of the story primarily due to the testimony of Norman Jeffries.

Around 10:00 p.m., Jeffries and his mother-in-law Eunice Murray were in Marilyn's house when Bobby Kennedy and two other men came to the door. This account agrees with that of Elizabeth Pollard, one of Marilyn's neighbors, who (as was her custom on Saturday nights) had friends over to play bridge; they saw Bobby Kennedy and two other men walk right past the window, headed for Marilyn's house, and one of the two men accompanying Bobby was carrying a small black bag of the sort that a doctor would carry.

According to Norman Jeffries, Bobby and the two mystery men entered the house and ordered Norman and Eunice to leave. Marilyn Monroe biographer Donald Wolfe quotes Norman as saying, "I mean they made it clear we were to be gone." This was the second time in one day that Bobby Kennedy had ordered them out of Marilyn's house. This time Bobby and friends obviously meant for them to go a considerable distance away somewhere and stay there, but Eunice and Norman only went to one of the neighbors' houses; Norman never specified which one, but they might well have gone to Hanna Fenichel's house, from which 12305 Fifth Helena Drive was visible. Eunice and Norman waited and watched, but saw nothing.

Nothing, that is, until they watched Bobby and his two companions leave Marilyn's house at about 10:30 p.m. and walk away into the night.

Convinced that the coast was clear, Eunice and Norman went back to the house, where, upon entering the property, they could hear Marilyn's dog Maf barking in the detached guest cottage to the left of the house proper. The guest cottage door was ajar, and they entered to find Marilyn sprawled face down, nude, across the day bed. She was alive, but she was dying. Jeffries said that her hand was "kind of holding the phone" and that her color was terrible. Eunice grabbed the phone out of Marilyn's hand and made two immediate calls– she called an ambulance, and she called Dr. Ralph Greenson. The latter told her to call Marilyn's physician, Dr. Hyman Engleberg.

Jeffries said that he went to the gate to wait for the ambulance, but before it got there, Peter Lawford's car pulled up, and Lawford and Marilyn's publicity agent Pat Newcomb got out. It isn't entirely clear why Lawford came over at that time– perhaps because Marilyn in her last moments of consciousness did put through a desperate-sounding call to him, or perhaps because

Eunice or someone else may have called him.

The arrival of Lawford and Newcomb near the time of Marilyn's death correlates well with Natalie Jacobs' account of her then fiancé Arthur Jacobs' receiving a call at the Hollywood Bowl concert from Pat Newcomb, but their arrival, as established by Norman Jeffries, puts the lie to just about everything Lawford and Newcomb themselves would say later on.

Not long before his death in 1984, Peter Lawford would tell an interviewer that he *should* have rushed right over to Marilyn's house upon (supposedly) getting her call and knowing that she was in trouble; Lawford, evidently still guilt-stricken, burst into tears upon saying this. But the fact is, he *did* rush over to Marilyn's house that night, a fact that he wasn't eager to have everyone know. The tears were real, but the reasons for them had more to do (I suspect) with remorse over his own part in the coverup than with simple regret over Marilyn's death. Lawford was entwined in the Kennedy family mystique, after all, and there were reputations to protect.

Also, Pat Newcomb's arrival with Peter Lawford shortly after 10:30 p.m., in time to make the phone call to her boss Arthur Jacobs, is at odds with her later statement that she first learned of Marilyn's death by way of a 4:00 a.m. phone call from Marilyn's attorney Mickey Rudin, who (Newcomb said, anyway) was at Marilyn's house at that hour. Newcomb, though she said she drove to Marilyn's house just after 4:00 a.m., is shown in news photos getting into Eunice Murray's car to leave, later on Sunday morning, and this was obviously because Peter Lawford had driven her there, so that her own car was still at his beach house.

Norman Jeffries recalled that Pat Newcomb, as soon as she got out of the car, became distraught and for some reason started yelling at Eunice. Later, neighbors would hear a hysterical woman screaming in the night: "You murderers! Are you satisfied now that she's dead?" Clearly, the screaming woman was Marilyn's "spin doctor" Pat Newcomb.

When the Shaefer Service ambulance arrived, driver James Hall and his partner rushed into the guest cottage and moved Marilyn onto the floor where they could apply a resuscitator. (Hall later said that in doing this, they dropped Marilyn "on her fanny," accounting for the bruises there that were noted in the autopsy.) The resuscitation procedure was actually going well; Marilyn's color was returning to normal.

But at this point a doctor came in, accompanied by two other men, and ordered the resuscitator removed. "Apply positive pressure," he ordered, and James Hall, knowing better than to argue with a doctor under such circumstances, began applying mouth-to-mouth resuscitation. The doctor meanwhile applied CPR, but according to Hall he did it incorrectly, pressing on Marilyn's abdomen rather than her chest. Presently he took a hypodermic syringe out of his bag, with a heart needle already attached. As an experienced paramedic, Hall thought it strange that the doctor had this ready to use, but again he thought it best not to say anything. The doctor, whom Hall distinctly heard mutter to himself, "I have to make a show out of this," made as if to insert the needle (presumably to inject adrenaline) into Marilyn's heart, but he put it in at the wrong angle and hit a rib. Correct medical procedure would obviously have been to back the needle out then and try again, but instead he leaned on the needle hard and cracked the rib, driving it into the heart.

Marilyn was dead, and years later James Hall, after describing this pseudomedical atrocity and (by way of hypnotic regression and police sketch techniques) identifying the doctor as Ralph Greenson, added the poignant colophon, "We had her saved."

Between the time Bobby Kennedy and his two cohorts entered Marilyn Monroe's house around 10:00 p.m. and the time they left it around 10:30 p.m., a loathsome crime was committed. Marilyn was clearly not expected to survive. But due to James Hall's resuscitation attempts, the deadly deed almost didn't come off. Dr. Greenson, by some apparently well-calculated bumbling, seems to have ensured that the work of those earlier visitors was not in vain. Whoever had actually given the fatal injection, Dr. Greenson did play a part later.

Hall, so instrumental in placing Greenson on the

scene, also later identified one of the men accompanying Greenson as Peter Lawford. It is significant that later that night, just before 12:00, an L.A. police patrolman named Lynn Franklin stopped a speeding car and was surprised to see that the driver was Peter Lawford and that one of the two men in the back seat was United States Attorney General Robert Kennedy. Looking at photographs later, Franklin was able to identify the other man as Dr. Ralph Greenson. Lawford explained to Officer Franklin that he was transporting the Attorney General to his hotel on important business. This was true, in a perverse sort of way– Lawford was basically helping get Bobby out of town. (Within the hour Bobby would be flown to San Francisco, where he would be safely back in his family's suite at the St. Francis Hotel, having checked in there on Friday, August 3rd.)

According to Norman Jeffries, when Marilyn died after Greenson's dubious ministrations, "all hell broke loose." There were numerous people coming in and out of the house all night, essentially "sanitizing " the place (my term, not Norman's) and arranging the "locked bedroom suicide" scenario later found by the police. Somewhere nearby, a helicopter hovered in the night. The house hummed with activity. Marilyn's attorney Mickey Rudin showed up at some point, as did officials from Twentieth Century Fox; the studio was concerned about the multi-million-dollar insurance policy it was keeping on Marilyn. But most of the people milling about seemed to be plainclothesmen or Secret Service types, according to Jeffries.

Marilyn's body was moved to her own bedroom, and her house was tidied up and rearranged. Wiretap and audio surveillance equipment were removed. When the regular forensics team checked the place out, later in the day, they found *no fingerprints*– not even Marilyn's. There should have been prints present in abundance, at the very least Marilyn's, Eunice's, Norman's, Pat Newcomb's, Bobby Kennedy's, Peter Lawford's, and Jeanne Carmen's. (Dust your own house for prints and see what you find.) Are we to believe that everyone who ever came into 12305 Fifth Helena Drive wore gloves? The place had been wiped clean, on someone's orders, to protect the guilty.

At length, at 4:25 that morning, after all parties concerned had had a chance to get their stories more or less straight, Dr. Hyman Engleberg called the West Los Angeles Police Department, identifying himself and saying, "Marilyn Monroe has committed suicide." Sergeant Jack Clemmons took the call and drove to the address given. When he arrived, he found Marilyn face-down on the bed in the regular bedroom, not in the guest cottage, since by now the body had been moved. He immediately got the impression that the body had been placed there, especially as the legs were straight, unlike the contorted position usually seen after a convulsive death.

When he asked the doctors (Greenson and Engleberg) if the body had been moved, they both said no, and this is highly significant, because as doctors they had the right to move the body and thus (in ordinary circumstances) no need to lie about it. But they *did* lie about it, suggesting again a pattern of orchestrated coverup and a covert motive strong enough to overrule both doctors' sense of professional ethics.

Sergeant Clemmons found Dr. Engleberg largely uncommunicative and Dr. Greenson oddly cocky and defiant. Greenson was quick to point to an empty Nembutal bottle on the bedside table, remarking, "She must have taken all of these." Clemmons made a note of the fact, however, that even after he had asked both doctors to help him look for a drinking glass, none was found.

After Dr. Engleberg said that he had declared Marilyn dead around 12:30 a.m. (he later said 3:50 a.m. when questioned by Sergeant Robert Byron), Clemmons asked both doctors why they had waited four hours (based on the 12:30 claim) to call the police. Greenson replied that they had had to wait until they got permission from the Twentieth Century Fox studio's publicity department before notifying the authorities of Marilyn's death.

The mind fairly reels at the absurdity of this statement. It is a legal requirement to report a death, and certainly the internal preferences of a movie studio would never take precedence over law. Even if the doctors *had* been required (which they decidedly were not) to seek permission from Fox, these were the pre-dawn hours on a Sunday morning; what were Engleberg and Greenson supposed to do, leave Marilyn lying there and wait till Monday morning and call the studio during business hours? A further question– if the publicity department at Fox really had to give permission for a doctor to report a death to the police, what if the publicity folks had refused permission? Would this have meant that Marilyn's death couldn't be reported at all? What it comes down to is that Dr. Ralph Greenson (to put it as delicately as I know how) was talking complete and utter bullshit.

As an integral part of the locked-bedroom-suicide scenario contrived at the scene, Dr. Greenson told Sergeant Clemmons that upon arriving at the house after being summoned by Eunice Murray, he looked through Marilyn's bedroom window from the yard and saw her lying nude on the bed. As Eunice (so the story went) had found the bedroom door locked, Greenson supposedly broke the glass, reached in and unlatched the window, crawled in, and unlocked the door. The problem with this is that, as Bob Slatzer pointed out a few days later, the broken glass from the bedroom window was scattered on the *outside*, not on the bedroom carpet, so that the window must have been broken from the inside. I would add that in the police photos of the broken window, the hole in the glass was barely big enough to put a hand through. Also, as Norman Mailer points out in his biography *Marilyn*, it is difficult to see how it could be true that Eunice Murray and Dr. Greenson had looked into Marilyn's bedroom through the window, since the drapes had been stapled down. Again, Greenson was lying. As was Eunice.

As were they all. Clemmons got the strong impression that everyone was mouthing lines that had been scripted for them, in a carefully rehearsed and orchestrated attempt at deception. He would in time come to understand, from the walls of silence he ran up against at every turn, that the coverup was a conspiracy encompassing not only the immediate witnesses but the L.A. Police Department, the District Attorney's office, the Coroner's office, and officials of the federal government as well. At any rate, Clemmons left the house that Sunday morning already firm in his opinion that the death he had just investigated was *not* a suicide.

Meanwhile, as the wind softly stirred the wind chimes (a gift from Carl Sandburg) in the yard of 12305 Fifth Helena Drive and a dismal piece of news began to circulate through the wire services, the California sun came up on a world without Marilyn Monroe. Shakespeare's Capulet might as well have been speaking of Norma Jeane, instead of Juliet, when he said, "Death lies on her like an untimely frost."

5.
The New Evidence: The Schulgen Connection

Marilyn's neighbor Elizabeth Pollard saw Bobby Kennedy and two other men (one carrying a little black medical bag) go into Marilyn's house that night, and Norman Jeffries vividly recalled the same kind of delegation arriving and ordering Eunice and him out of the house. Norman saw Bobby and the two companions come out of the house half an hour later and walk away. In between, Marilyn was injected with a massive, many-times-over deadly dose of pentobarbital and chloral hydrate.

Attorney General Bobby Kennedy clearly was present at the time of the lethal injection. He probably didn't give the injection itself, indeed probably didn't know how to use a hypodermic needle, at least not deftly enough to give a shot for which the autopsist Thomas Noguchi missed finding the needle mark. But he was there, and he apparently did nothing to stand in the way of Marilyn's execution. (One has to ask: was he present against his will, *forced* to watch someone kill Marilyn? One is not overwhelmed by any sense that this is likely.) Biographer Donald Wolfe, in *The Last Days of Marilyn Monroe*, pulls no punches about this: "The evidence points to premeditated homicide. In the presence of Bobby Kennedy, [Marilyn] was injected with enough barbiturates to kill fifteen people."

But the notion that John and Robert Kennedy were involved in the circumstances of Marilyn's death began to circulate as early as 1964, when Frank Capell suggested as much in his book *The Strange Death of Marilyn Monroe*, published by Capell's own Herald of Freedom, an anti-communist group. Capell's take on this whole thing was that the Kennedys, somehow in league with communists, brought about Marilyn's demise. It is clear now, however, that the direct motives behind Marilyn's murder had, ideologically, nothing to do with that old bugaboo of the mid-twentieth century, communism, despite the fact that the surveillance on Marilyn (and her leftist acquaintances) clearly had a lot to do with the communist scare of those days.

No, the *motive* was simply to shut Marilyn up about secrets that John Kennedy imparted to her, and that forces within the government of the United States were (and are) eager to keep covered up. Capell's book attracted little attention at the time, but over the years other investigators have made it known that Capell was right, at least in saying that the Kennedys were implicated, if not for the ideological reasons with which Capell was obsessed.

While this connection to the Kennedys is not new, it has only been suggested that the Kennedy motives were UFO-coverup-related since the surfacing, in the mid-1990s, of a remarkable CIA document dated August 3, 1962, the day before Marilyn's death. And as we shall see, even this document isn't the whole story– but something connected with it constitutes the new and startling piece of evidence of which I seek to make the public aware.

The manner in which this document came to be known is a little tricky to follow. Timothy Cooper, an investigator trained by the Nick Harris Detective Academy, received the document from someone he understood to be a former CIA archivist. Cooper passed the document along to Milo Speriglio (head of the Nick Harris Detective Agency), and together they publicized the document sufficiently to generate a special on the Fox television program *Encounters* (1994) and an article in *UFO Magazine* (1995). If indeed the provider of the document was an archivist, it is understandable that the source is unnamed, because the designations of TOP SECRET on the document were never marked out, as they would have been by standard practice if the document had actually been declassified and released in the normal way. The document was apparently obtained without being *released* in the usual sense of

-55-

CENTRAL INTELLIGENCE AGENCY

NOT FOR PUBLICATION

COUNTRY: New York, US
SUBJECT: Marilyn Monroe
DATE: 3 August 1962
REFERENCES: ROCK DUNE Project

Wiretap of telephone conversation between reporter Dorothy Kilgallen and close friend, Howard Rothberg (A); from wiretap of telephone conversation of Marilyn Monroe and Attorney General Robert Kennedy (B). Appraisal of Contents:

1. Rothberg discussed the apparent behavior of subject with Kilgallen and the break up with the Kennedys. Rothberg told Kilgallen that she was attending Hollywood parties hosted by the "inner circle" among Hollywood's elite and was becoming the talk of the town again. Rothberg indicated in so many words, that she had secrets to tell, no doubt arising from her trysts with the President and the Attorney General. One such "secret" mentions the visit by the President at a secret air base for the purpose of inspecting things from outer space. Kilgallen replied that she knew what might be the source of visit. In the mid-fifties Kilgallen learned of secret effort by US and UK governments to identify the origins of crashed spacecraft and dead bodies, from a British government official. Kilgallen believed the story may have come from the New York Journal in the late forties. Kilgallen said that if the story is true, it would cause terrible embarrassment to Jack and his plans to have NASA put men on the moon.

2. Subject repeatedly called the Attorney General and complained about the way she was being ignored by the President and his brother.

3. Subject threatened to hold a press conference and would tell all.

4. Subject made reference to "bases" in Cuba and knew of the President's plan to kill Castro.

5. Subject made reference to her "diary of secrets" and what the newspapers would do with such disclosures.

TOP SECRET

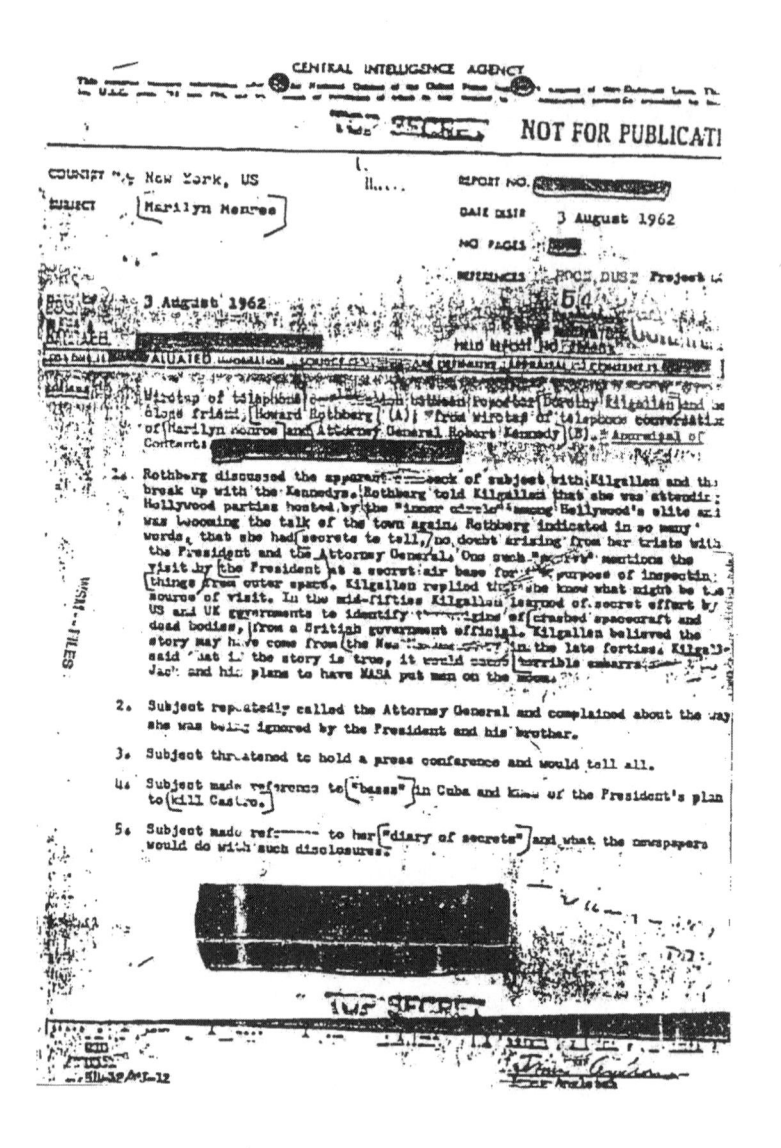

The Marilyn Monroe
CIA Document

the term. But however it happened, the appearance of this document is one of the most significant breakthroughs in the history of investigation of government-directed coverup activities.

Dr. Steven Greer, director of the CSETI (Center for the Study of Extraterrestrial Intelligence) Disclosure Project group, says in his book *Extraterrestrial Contact: The Evidence and Implications* that the Marilyn Monroe document came to him in 1994 "by way of a contact with access to NSA officials." He further states, with reference to the question of the document's genuineness: "It has been authenticated by the best document researcher in the world– a man who for years sat outside General Odom's door as his senior aide when Odom was NSA head." (Retired General William E. Odom was Director of the National Security Agency from 1985 to 1989. When I asked the Steven Greer group, in September 2002, who General Odom's "senior aide" was, they told me that the aide prefers not to be identified.) It would appear that at some point the Cooper-Speriglio group passed the document around inclusively enough to have it absorbed into what Dr. Greer calls the "Project Starlight paper trail." (Project Starlight is CSETI's effort to bring about official disclosure on the matter of extraterrestrial intelligence.)

The document, with a standard Central Intelligence Agency heading, bears a subject line reading "Marilyn Monroe" and a project line reading

"Moon Dust." Interestingly enough, various military and government agencies have for years denied (to Clifford Stone and other researchers) that Project Moon Dust ever existed, but in fact existing documentation makes it perfectly clear that Project Moon Dust (whose classified name, once compromised, has now been replaced with some other designation) does exist, and has existed at least since 1953, for the purpose of recovering debris from fallen space vehicles, certainly to include UFO crash debris. An intriguing and problematical project line, certainly, to find on a CIA document about Marilyn Monroe.

Another suggestive feature of the document is an apparent reference, in the routing data at the bottom of the page, to MJ-12. This allusion to Majestic Twelve (the group, ever controversial in the field of UFO studies, reportedly formed by President Truman after the crash at Roswell in 1947 to oversee UFO-related matters) further associates the Marilyn Monroe document with the whole question of governmental secrecy about unidentified flying objects. When I interviewed him on September 14, 1999, Roswell crash retrieval witness Frank Kaufmann assured me MJ-12 did exist, though he said it was a kind of façade or front-organization, much like the Air Force's Project Blue Book. And assuming that there really was, whatever its nature, such an organization as MJ-12, the point here is that the routing of a document about Marilyn Monroe and the official

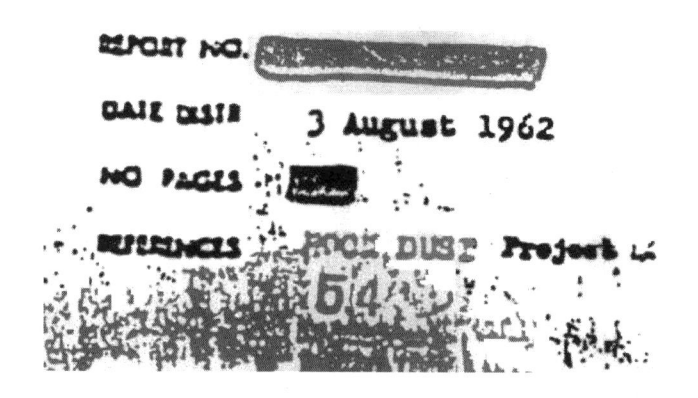

The Project MOON DUST designation in the Marilyn Monroe document.

The apparent reference to MJ-12 in the routing data on the Marilyn Monroe CIA document.

secrets that she may have known, to such a group, tends again to imply a connection between the Marilyn Monroe matter and the whole question of UFO secrecy. The body of the document, which is only slightly obscured by redaction (blacking out), reads as follows:

> *[Near the top of the page, the report number and the number of pages are redacted.]*
> Wiretap of telephone conversation between reporter Dorothy Kilgallen and her close friend, Howard Rothberg (A); from wiretap of telephone conversation of Marilyn Monroe and Attorney General Robert Kennedy (B). Appraisal of Content: *[A portion redacted.]*
>
> 1. Rothberg discussed the apparent comeback of subject with Kilgallen and the break up with the Kennedys. Rothberg told Kilgallen that she was attending Hollywood parties hosted by the "inner circle" among Hollywood's elite and was becoming the talk of the town again. Rothberg indicated in so many words, that she had secrets to tell, no doubt arising from her trists *[sic]* with the President and the Attorney General. One such "secret" mentions the visit by the President at a secret air base for the purpose of inspecting things from outer space. Kilgallen replied that she knew what might be the source of visit. In the mid-fifties Kilgallen learned of secret effort by US and UK governments to identify the origins of crashed spacecraft and dead bodies, from a British government official. Kilgallen believed the story

may have come from the New Mexico story in the late forties. Kilgallen said that if the story is true, it would cause terrible embarrassment for Jack and his plans to have NASA put men on the moon.

2. Subject repeatedly called the Attorney General and complained about the way she was being ignored by the President and his brother.

3. Subject threatened to hold a press conference and would tell all.

4. Subject made reference to "bases" in Cuba and knew of the President's plan to kill Castro.

5. Subject made reference to her "diary of secrets" and what the newspapers would do with such disclosures.

[An indented block of text is redacted near the bottom of the page, and the document is signed JAMES ANGLETON. Angleton at the time was the Chief of Counterintelligence for the CIA.]

The reference to Marilyn's "diary of secrets" makes it clear that the government was highly concerned about what she might know, and what she might have written down– state secrets derived from Jack and Bobby Kennedy. And certainly the reference to one secret's being "the visit by the President to a secret air base for the purpose of inspecting things from outer space" makes it abundantly clear what specific classified information they were afraid she might have written about.

Whether she actually had written about it or not, Marilyn knew about UFO-related secrets that (from the reference to Dorothy Kilgallen) were related to "the New Mexico story in the late forties" and were imparted to her by the President. (Dorothy Kilgallen herself died mysteriously on November 8, 1965; she was working on a book about the John Kennedy assassination, a book supposed to contain "explosive information," and her manuscript and notes all disappeared.)

The natural, indeed well-nigh ineluctable, inference from the CIA document is that Marilyn knew about the crash and retrieval of a flying saucer in the New Mexico desert.

Marilyn knew about Roswell. The document suggesting as much is dated "3 August 1962," and the next day Marilyn was dead.

Given this insight, with regard to Marilyn's probable awareness of the Top Secret Roswell affair, one will find it easy to understand the official *angst* over the little red diary. It's easy to understand, too, why Bobby Kennedy threw the diary across the room; easy to understand why, on the surveillance tapes at Marilyn's house, Bobby could be heard raving like a lunatic as he searched for the diary.

Bobby had long been in the habit of playing protector to his wayward brother Jack, and now the stakes were very high. Whatever the diary really contained, the important concern was what the Kennedys thought it *might* contain.

The big question of course is– what ever happened to Marilyn's diary? Its ultimate destination is a mystery, but at least we know what happened to it during the two or three days following Marilyn's death. She often kept it locked in the four-drawer file cabinet in her guest cottage, and apparently it remained there at least until Monday morning, August 6. On that morning Coroner's Aide Lionel Grandison sent his driver to Marilyn's house to try to find an address book so that relatives could be notified. The driver found Eunice Murray at the house, since Eunice had come over to open the house for Marilyn's executrix Inez Melson. Eunice gave the driver an address book and a little red diary, both of which the driver delivered to Grandison at the Los Angeles County Coroner's Office.

After examining the diary briefly and noting that while it contained interesting references to the Kennedys and other people (notably Fidel Castro), it contained no addresses, Grandison, before leaving for the day, locked the diary in the safe in the Coroner's office. When he came back to work on Tuesday morning, August 7, the safe was still locked, but when he opened it he saw that the diary was gone. Very few people knew the combination to the safe, and my best surmise is that Dr. Theodore Curphey, the Los Angeles

County Coroner, removed the diary during the night of August 6-7 and passed it along to whoever was demanding it. Curphey is known to have falsified and removed records, no doubt on behalf of governmental figures who needed to manipulate the facts to protect themselves, and it would be reasonable to assume that he delivered Marilyn's little red "book of secrets" to officials of the CIA or the Justice Department. To this day, no one (at least no one without access to exceedingly highly classified information) knows for sure where the diary is.

    In any case, the whole matter assumes a new character in light of an important discovery that I had the good fortune to make about the CIA document itself.

    At the time of this writing I am, and have been for several years, the director of one of the computer labs on campus at Eastern New Mexico University in Roswell. One day during the Spring 2001 semester I had the Marilyn Monroe CIA document displayed on a computer screen in my office in the lab. I was essentially looking at the wording of the document and at its markings and routing data, where as mentioned the references to Moon Dust and MJ-12 were sufficiently intriguing to ponder. At this point Jane Shoemaker, a student worker in my lab, pointed to a place on the document just to the left of the TOP SECRET stamp near the top and remarked that there appeared to be a sort of smudge or shadow, as if something had been typed there. I hadn't noticed it myself, but I could see that Jane was right. Something *was* there. It was little more than a vague imprint, and neither she nor I nor any of the other people standing nearby could make out what it was.

But one of my specialties is computer image enhancement. It didn't take long, and didn't require anything more than some simple imaging techniques, to make the vague smudge atop the Marilyn Monroe memo readable. I will forever be grateful to Jane for noticing that something was there, because the connection it establishes has turned out to be of immense importance– a discovery that links the Marilyn Monroe problem, more squarely than ever before, to the whole field of UFO studies, the whole matter of UFO secrecy and government coverups.

What I discovered is that the imprint (or bleed-in, or whatever one might call it) contains the name Schulgen, a name I immediately recognized. I must admit, I nearly fell off my chair when I saw it.

The imprint says (just below the regular "Central Intelligence Agency" heading) "EXHIBIT B." A little further down, it says, "GEN. SCHULGEN INTELLIGENCE COLLECTION MEMORANDUM–19...." A little further down: "This exhibit includes the Intelligence Collection Memorandum...." A little further

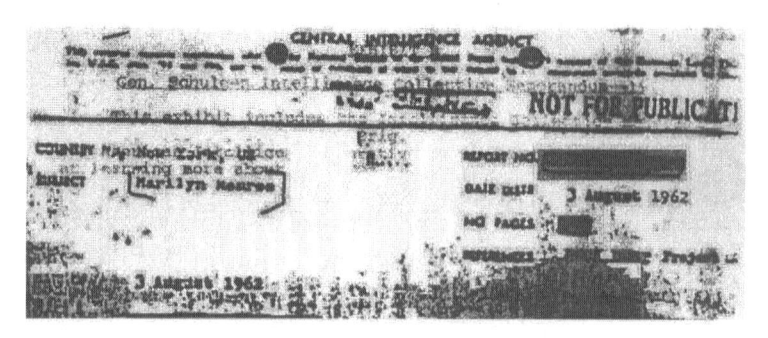

The "Schulgen" imprint on the top of the Marilyn Monroe CIA memo

down again, there is more, but here we find only isolated fragments of text: "Brig.," "tiv," "at learning more about." Under the document's "Country: New York, US" there is a fragmentary imprint, difficult to read, that appears possibly to say "American Intelligence." All in all, though, there is enough to establish the crucial connection, because Brigadier General George Schulgen is plainly indicated. (I should mention that in earlier published appearances of the CIA document– e.g. in Hesemann and Mantle's *Beyond Roswell,* Wolfe's *The Last Days of Marilyn Monroe,* and Greer's *Extraterrestrial Contact*– the "Schulgen" imprint is invisible.)

Brigadier General George Schulgen, during the time following the Roswell UFO crash and retrieval of 1947, was Chief of the Air Intelligence Requirements

Division of Army Air Corps Intelligence. Basically, his job for the Army Air Corps, and then for the Air Force when it became a separate branch of the military in late 1947, was coördination of the investigation of "flying disks," as they were then often called. The Intelligence Collection Memorandum referred to in the fragmentary text that I discovered to be imprinted on the CIA document is an actual memorandum that had been circulated in the intelligence community by General Schulgen on October 28, 1947 for the purpose of describing and justifying intelligence information being collected about flying saucers. (Dr. Bruce Maccabee discusses this particular document in detail in his book *UFO FBI Connection.*)

There exists an internal FBI memo (addressed to special agent D. M. Ladd, subject "Flying Disks") dated July 10, 1947 discussing General Schulgen's request (the previous day, five days after the Roswell UFO incident) that the FBI help the Army Air Corps investigate flying saucers and sighting witnesses. This document states, in part:

> General Schulgen advised [*name redacted*] that the possibility exists that the first reported sightings of the so-called flying disks were fallacious and prompted by individuals seeking personal publicity, or were reported for political reasons. He stated that if this was so, subsequent sightings might be the result of a mass hysteria. He pointed out that the thought

exists that the first reported sightings might have been by individuals of Communist sympathies with the view to causing hysteria and fear of a secret Russian weapon. . . . he desired the assistance of the Federal Bureau of Investigation in locating and questioning the individuals who first sighted the so-called flying disks in order to ascertain whether or not they are sincere in their statements. . . . General Schulgen assured [*name redacted*] that there are no War Department or Navy Department research projects presently being conducted which could in any way be tied up with the flying disks. General Schulgen indicated to [*name redacted*] that if the Bureau would cooperate with him in this matter, he would offer all the facilities of his office as to the results obtained in the effort to identify and run down this matter.

How much General Schulgen's office at Wright Field (later Wright-Patterson Air Force Base) knew about flying saucers this soon after the Roswell crash is difficult to say, so Schulgen may or may not have been playing some games here with the FBI, but in any event it is obvious that he was up to his ears in flying-saucer-related concerns. How the "Schulgen" imprint or bleed-in got on the CIA document about Marilyn Monroe isn't clear– it may possibly have been a show-through in photocopying or scanning, for example, or a digital palimpsest of some kind– but the implication in any case is that *the Marilyn Monroe CIA document and an exhibit ("Exhibit B") containing the Schulgen Intelligence Collection Memorandum were archived together* in some highly secret government-agency file.

This revelation, which I am calling "the Schulgen connection," establishes a solid link between the UFO coverup and what ended up happening to Marilyn. The CIA document alone would have strongly suggested as much, but the "Schulgen" imprint really drives the point home.

In light of all this, it becomes increasingly clear what happened to Marilyn and why.

I should perhaps mention that the first thing I did, upon discovering the Schulgen connection, was to publish an article about it in the MUFON (Mutual UFO Network) *UFO Journal*– the May 2001 issue– for my own safety, and Jane Shoemaker's. In this business, it sometimes isn't a good idea to be the only one who knows something.

Let me formalize, now, what I have been leading up to.

6.
The Crucial Hypothesis: Marilyn, JFK, and UFOs

What is a hypothesis?

In the field of UFO studies, as in any other field of reasoned inquiry, a hypothesis is *an educated conjecture that, if true, would best account for the observed facts.* Such a conjecture, once it has been seen to explain the known facts best, comes to be regarded as true, or as having a high probability of being true, until a better hypothesis– one better able to explain the facts– comes along, if it ever does.

For example, we have observed arroyos (dry river beds) on the surface of Mars. The hypothesis that best explains the existence of these arroyos is that there were once rivers on Mars. Other hypotheses– e.g., that the river beds were deliberately dug by shovel-wielding bands of Martian pixies, or that the river beds were placed there by Satan to confuse us– are not capable of accounting for *all* the known facts so well as the hypothesis that Mars once had rivers, especially when the known facts include, for example, the fact that the atmosphere of Mars has become too thin to keep water on the surface of Mars in liquid form, and the fact that ice is known to exist at the Martian polar caps. If another hypothesis comes along that is better, then so be it– but until then, we assume that active rivers once coursed across the sandy surface of the Red Planet.

The order of operations, then is: (1) collect and study pieces of factual information, and (2) formulate the best hypothesis to account for them. We have collected and analyzed information about the Marilyn Monroe problem. Now let's formulate a

HYPOTHESIS:

During his romantic encounters with Marilyn Monroe, President John F. Kennedy imparted state secrets to her, including his knowledge of at least one UFO crash and retrieval, probably from the Roswell, New Mexico incident; subsequently, because of her developing annoyance with both John Kennedy and Attorney General Robert Kennedy, Marilyn was expressly determined to hold a press conference, and (characteristically protective of his brother) Robert Kennedy, fearing that her public revelations might conceivably include the secret of secrets, first tried to reason with her and then, when that failed, directed that she be silenced by a lethal injection of barbiturates; thus Marilyn Monroe died, a murder victim, because government officials recoiled at the consequences of her possible public disclosure of what she knew about the official coverup of unidentified flying objects.

We have examined a good bit of evidence already– Marilyn's toxicology report, proving that her death could not have been suicide; witness accounts that place Bobby Kennedy and his associates at the murder scene; witness accounts that reveal a concerted effort to conspire to make Marilyn's time of death seem to have been hours later than it really was; a history of sex-related indiscretions and security lapses on JFK's part; a CIA document expressing official anxiety over Marilyn's "secrets," one of which had to do with the President's knowledge of "things from outer space"; an imprint on that document mentioning General Schulgen, one of the Air Force's primary UFO-investigation coördinators.

One species of evidence of which I have made mention only in passing is the matter of the surveillance tapes, both those derived from wiretaps of Marilyn's phones and those derived from audio surveillance "bugs" placed in her house. (Both governmental and private parties had her under surveillance.) As we have seen, the audio surveillance tapes (from the testimony of a former government official who had heard them) revealed Bobby Kennedy to have been in a nearly psychotic fit of anger at Marilyn's house that Saturday afternoon. But there is a more chilling bit of evidence from the private-sector wiretap tapes, part of which Marilyn's longtime friend Robert Slatzer was allowed to hear. These tapes, produced by West Coast investigator Fred Otash apparently at the behest of East Coast "master spy" and wiretap expert Bernie Spindel, were in the possession of Spindel until December 15, 1966, when New York District Attorney Frank Hogan– a friend and political ally of Bobby Kennedy's– staged an early-morning raid at Spindel's upstate New York house and confiscated all the Marilyn Monroe materials. This, by the way, was illegal, because Hogan's warrant called only for the confiscation of wiretap equipment, *not* surveillance tapes. But Spindel never got them back, and in fact died during the legal battle he staged to try to do so.

Slatzer, in his book *The Marilyn Files*, describes hearing portions of the audio surveillance tapes on which Bobby Kennedy and Peter Lawford at some point (the tape seemed to have been edited to condense the empty passage of time, and I surmise that this portion would have been recorded at Peter Lawford's house) could be heard making plans to the effect that Bobby would get out of Los Angeles that night and call Lawford from San Francisco to check on the success of the coverup. On part of the wiretap tapes definitely derived from Lawford's house, Slatzer could hear Bobby's voice on the line– after an operator said that a long distance call was coming in from the Bay area– asking Lawford,

"Is she dead?"

If this sounds fanciful, let us consider a Federal Bureau of Investigation memo– one of unquestionable provenance, as I downloaded it from the FBI Web site itself– bearing a date stamp of October 23, 1964 and describing the same exchange between Bobby Kennedy and Peter Lawford. The document is four pages long, counting a cover page that says that the document was forwarded to the Bureau by "[*name redacted*], former Special Agent, who is currently Field Representative, Appointment Section, Governor's Office, State of California." The cover sheet also says that the unnamed Special Agent "cannot evaluate the authenticity of this information," but one has to suppose that Special Agents do not routinely pass information along to the Bureau without some sense that that information is valid.

I can do no better than to allow the FBI document to speak for itself. Besides stating that "[o]n the day that Marilyn died, Bobby Kennedy was in town, and registered at the Beverly Hills Hotel," the document tells us:

> On the day of Marilyn's death, Robert Kennedy checked out of the Beverly Hills Hotel and flew from Los Angeles International Airport via Western Airlines to San Francisco, where he checked into the St. Francis Hotel. The owner of this hotel is a Mr. London, a friend of Robert Kennedy. Robert Kennedy made a telephone call from St. Charles

Hotel, San Francisco, to Peter Lawford to find out if Marilyn was dead yet. Peter Lawford had called Marilyn's number and spoken with her, and then checked again later to make sure she did not answer.

This correlates perfectly with Robert Slatzer's account of the surveillance and wiretap tapes he listened to. (Others heard these tapes too, including Bernie Spindel's technician Earl Jaycox, and have given consistent accounts of their contents.)

The document, further down, goes on to say, of Marilyn's psychiatrist– Ralph Greenson, though he is unnamed here– and with reference to the time immediately following her death:

> He made contact with the coroner and an arrangement was made for a psychiatric board of inquiry to be appointed by the coroner, an unheard of procedure in the area. This was so the findings could be recorded that she was emotionally unbalanced. It was reported this arrangement was to discredit any statements she may have made before she died.

As someone has so colorfully observed, the more you stir it, the more it stinks.

Since it is obvious that Marilyn was under surveillance, and equally obvious that the results of the surveillance (including the wiretaps at Peter Lawford's beach house) were spectacular, I put in a Freedom of

Information Act (FOIA) letter on October 1, 2001 to the CIA, requesting

> a copy of the transcripts of any and all wiretaps done by or for the CIA, on both of the telephones of actress Marilyn Monroe for the dates of Saturday, 4 August 1962 and Sunday, 5 August 1962, on the following numbers at her residence at 12305 Fifth Helena Drive, Brentwood, California: GRanite 2-4830, GRanite 6-1890.

I cited the August 3, 1962 CIA document as indication from the CIA itself that she was under wiretap surveillance, and attached a copy of the document, both here and in subsequent correspondence, thus giving the CIA every opportunity to disavow the document; they did not do so. What they did do was to assign the request the case reference number F-2001-02071, and their reply, dated October 31, 2001, said:

> Concerning your request, please be advised that we have completed thorough and diligent searches on behalf of previous requesters for information pertaining to this subject and no responsible records were located.

This is essentially form-letter boilerplate language, and needless to say I was less than satisfied with their response. On December 10, 2001 I submitted an appeal, again attaching the famous CIA memo and citing Marilyn's left-wing associations in Mexico as establishing the theoretical propriety, within the CIA charter, of their having placed Marilyn under surveillance, a surveillance of which there must be records at the Agency.

The CIA could simply have rejected this appeal, but they didn't. They did overrun their time limit of twenty working days, and I sent them a noncompliance letter on March 9, 2002. They responded with a letter dated May 1, 2002 stating, "Your appeal has been accepted and arrangements will be made for its consideration by the appropriate members of the Agency Release Panel. You will be advised of the determinations made." (By accepting my appeal, by the way, which was based on the Marilyn Monroe memo, the CIA itself tacitly validated the memo for me.)

Simultaneously, I went through exactly the same FOIA request procedure with regard to obtaining a photocopy of Marilyn's long-vanished little red diary, to which request they assigned the case reference number F-2001-02070. My original FOIA request letter, appeal letter, and noncompliance letter (all with regard to the diary) were sent on the same dates as the wiretap transcript request letters. The CIA sent its initial response ("no responsible records were located") and its appeal-acceptance letter on the same dates as in the other case.

But they responded to the diary appeal first, in a letter dated July 16, 2002, stating that the members of the Agency Release Panel "have advised that the processing of your request has been reconsidered and the results reconfirmed: no responsible documents were located."

I didn't receive a response to my wiretap transcript appeal until about a month after the response on the diary appeal, when a letter dated August 19, 2002 arrived, with essentially the same form-letter boilerplate language: with regard to my request for transcripts of wiretaps on Marilyn's phones at the time of her death, the Agency Release Panel had reconsidered the matter and reaffirmed the CIA's earlier claim that "no responsive documents were located."

This has to be a lie.

The CIA's own "Marilyn Monroe" memo of August 3, 1962 plainly *says* that the CIA had access to the contents of wiretap surveillance on Marilyn. The CIA, we may be sure, keeps records. It follows that their claim now *not* to have such records is untrue. The logic of all this is strange, too– if there were no existing records, why did they *accept* my appeal and send the whole matter to the Agency Release Panel to deliberate whether to release documents to me, only to come back and say that it was as they thought, there were no records to release?

But then what else *could* they say? By law, under the Freedom of Information Act, if an agency of the federal government admits to *having* a document but declines to release it, that agency must specify, to the requester, precisely which of the nine legal exemptions justifies their refusal to release the material. (I am always careful to mention this in any FOIA request for documents.) In the case of wiretaps on Marilyn's phones, given the sensitive nature of things that she knew about as suggested by the August 3, 1962 CIA memo itself, the exemption that no doubt would have been necessary for them to cite is Exemption One, the exemption concerning national security information. Obviously if the CIA were to tell me or any investigator that Marilyn's wiretap transcripts existed but were being withheld due to "national security," the embarrassing question would be: what could Marilyn have known in 1962 that was not only classified then, but is *still* classified several decades later, still a matter of "national security"?

What indeed, if not a UFO-related secret?

We don't know whether Marilyn's diary actually contained an account of UFO secrets, but it's abundantly clear that the CIA was concerned that it might. Also we don't know whether the CIA in fact has the diary. I suspect they do, but it's possible that Theodore Curphey, the L.A. Coroner, may have given it to Robert Kennedy, and from there, who knows?

The existing evidence strongly supports the hypothesis I have stated. But there still remains one highly important piece of evidence to examine.

7.

Clincher:
The Bolaños Interview

In February of 1962, shortly after moving into her house at 12305 Fifth Helena Drive in Brentwood, California, Marilyn took a trip to Mexico and met, among other people, the twenty-six-year-old Mexican film director and screenwriter José Bolaños. They were immediately attracted to each other. Depending on whom you talk to, Marilyn either was or wasn't serious about him; some of her associates have suggested that she may even have been thinking about marrying him, though others say it wasn't that serious. But Bolaños did follow her back to Los Angeles and in fact escorted her to the Golden Globe Awards in March 1962.

The important thing here is that Bolaños called Marilyn around 10:00 p.m. on the night of August 4, 1962, less than an hour before she died.

In 1983, twenty-one years after that telephone conversation, Anthony Summers interviewed José Bolaños. I am convinced that neither Summers nor anyone else has realized, until now, how important that interview was, because of something Marilyn said to Bolaños just before she was to die.

Bolaños told Anthony Summers that Marilyn told him "something shocking– something that will one day shock the whole world."

Keep in mind, again, that this interview took place in 1983, twenty-one years after Marilyn's death. Yet Bolaños vividly remembered the conversation in stark detail and– most importantly– used the *future tense,* saying, in 1983, that Marilyn told him something that would sooner or later shock the whole world but had not yet done so. This had to be something, then, *that had still not come out publicly in 1983,* and, one gathers, never *has* come out officially.

Again the question is: what did Marilyn know in 1962 that was still secret and potentially "shocking" in 1983? Our hypothesis here, that JFK had told her UFO-related, extraterrestrial-contact-related matters of high secrecy, would answer this question very solidly.

John Kennedy had of course told Marilyn other state secrets as well. According to the August 3, 1962 CIA memo, Marilyn knew, for example, about the President's plan to assassinate Fidel Castro. But by 1983 none of these other matters that Marilyn knew about were still secret. In contrast, the UFO crash retrieval information she evidently knew about still *was* classified, and may well always be.

Much has been said about Marilyn's affairs with both Jack and Bobby Kennedy, and one might entertain an alternative hypothesis to the effect that what Marilyn told José Bolaños about, that night on the phone, was her affairs with the Kennedy brothers. But this is scarcely a realistic hypothesis. By 1983 much had already become known, long since, about Marilyn and the Kennedys, and besides, Bolaños would hardly consider these romantic dalliances to be something that would "one day shock the whole world." Bolaños, an accomplished "ladies' man" himself, would not be so naive as to suppose that the "whole world"– already settled into the modern cynical and street-wise mode by 1983– would find such things "shocking."

No, Marilyn must have told him something far more spectacular than that. Little wonder, then, that the CIA has (twice) lied to me about the wiretap transcripts, saying that no such records can be found. Clearly, a transcript of exactly what Marilyn said that Saturday night to José Bolaños would be a stunning document, if it were open to public scrutiny. Bolaños wouldn't tell Anthony Summers what it was that Marilyn said to him, and I hoped to interview Bolaños myself, but, alas, learned that he died in Mexico City on June 11, 1994 at the age of only 58.

The central hypothesis here– that Marilyn knew about governmental secrets relating to UFOs and ended up dying for it, best explains the implications of the Bolaños interview.

We are in a position now to observe how the various facets of evidence *correlate* with each other. Correlated evidence is always better than isolated facts, and in this case the evidence correlates very well, essentially eliminating alternatives to our hypothesis.

One might list six points of evidence and see how they appear when examined not in isolation but together:

(1) The CIA memo of August 3, 1962.
(2) The "Schulgen" imprint on the CIA memo.
(3) The Marilyn Monroe toxicology report.
(4) The witness accounts of the circumstances surrounding Marilyn's death.
(5) The hysterical behavior of Robert Kennedy.
(6) The Bolaños interview.

These points interact in a number of different ways, and while none of them alone would make the whole case, together they do. For example, an alternative conclusion might be that when the CIA memo refers to the President's examination of "things from outer space," that phrase might have referred to Russian experimental spacecraft debris recovered at some point by the U.S. military. But in light of the "Schulgen" imprint, it could scarcely mean that— remember, Schulgen was one of the Air Force's top UFO people. Also, such a lesser interpretation would not account for all the anxiety generated by the whole scenario, as illustrated by Bobby Kennedy's hysterical ravings on the surveillance tapes, and by the tone of the CIA memo itself.

Some people have theorized that Bobby's histrionic behavior at Marilyn's house may have had to do with his anxiety that his wife would know about his affair with Marilyn. But this argument makes no sense, because Ethel Kennedy already knew about it, just as Jackie Kennedy was perfectly aware of JFK's indiscretions. Further, as we have observed, the "something that will one day shock the whole world" from the Bolaños interview could not be something so relatively innocuous as the brothers' affairs with (yet another) movie star, not in a world grown jaded enough to pay only passing attention to such things. Also it seems highly unlikely that Bobby and Jack were simply worried about their political futures with regard to possible public knowledge of their bedroom antics. For anyone good enough at manipulation (of money and people and blocks of influence), elections– indeed the Electoral College itself– can be picked up and played like a violin, and nobody was ever better at this than the Kennedy family. They could behave like Attila the Hun and still keep getting elected, and they knew it.

What do all the witness accounts imply? The whole effect at Marilyn's house that night was to give the impression (1) that Marilyn committed suicide and

(2) that it happened several hours after Marilyn and Bobby had been together. But on the first point, both the toxicology report and the various witness assessments of Marilyn's moods show that she couldn't have killed herself; and on the second point, witnesses placed Bobby at the house *at the very time* of Marilyn's death, so that his angry tirade on Saturday afternoon wasn't a resolved episode (or an episode in which Bobby simply left her forever, disgusted with her)– Bobby returned to the house that night, having failed to placate (or intimidate) Marilyn in the afternoon.

Likewise, even though the toxicology report leaves it *conceivable* (however unlikely) that Marilyn could have given herself the lethal injection, the testimony of her friends shows that she would hardly have been either inclined to do so or capable of doing so. (She was in good spirits, looking forward to the future. And she didn't own or know how to use a hypodermic needle.)

Much depends on the Bolaños interview and its "something shocking," and while this *could* have been something other than Marilyn's talking about UFO-related secrets, one needs to think about the Bolaños interview in the light of other evidence– in this case, the CIA memo and its very telling "Schulgen" imprint. Our hypothesis, that it all goes back to the UFO question, best accounts for the interview and its "something that will one day shock the whole world."

Again, the information is best when viewed as *interrelated*. What we really have, in all these points of evidence, is a kind of "intertext" that tells us an organically whole and connected tale. And heaven knows, it isn't a pretty picture.

What we need to do here, finally, is to think through all the implications of these facets of evidence in terms of Attorney General Robert Kennedy's frame of mind that fateful weekend. How did he see his possible choices, his viable options?

It isn't hard to figure out pretty much what he must have been thinking, and what he finally resolved that he had to do.

8.

The Press Conference that Never Was

As the CIA memo of August 3, 1962 makes clear, Marilyn Monroe was exceedingly annoyed with the Kennedy brothers and was promising to hold a press conference and "tell all."

It's too bad Marilyn didn't just go ahead and *have* a press conference. Unfortunately, she committed the fatal error of talking about it first on the phone. If she had just held a press conference without warning those with the motive and the power to stop her, everything would have been different.

Everything. *Very* different.

Marilyn would have lived, and that would have made the world a better place, in many ways, than it has otherwise been since 1962. But the immediate picture, on a national scale, certainly wouldn't have been very nice.

Little or nothing has ever been said or written about what *might* have happened if Marilyn had stepped up to those microphones that Monday morning.

Who knows– maybe she would only have said, "These guys slept with me, and promised to divorce their wives and marry me, and now they've dropped me to save their own sorry political asses." The Kennedys could have lived with that. As we have observed, getting elected was never a problem for the Kennedy clan; even Teddy, after the Chappaquiddick scandal, never had any trouble staying in the United States Senate, and both Jack and Bobby led similarly charmed lives, or thought they did. (Needless to say, their assassinations were tragic– even for people who are as reprehensible as these guys were, getting shot shouldn't ever be in the cards.)

But what if Marilyn had other things in mind for the press conference?

I have endeavored to put myself in Bobby Kennedy's place, to think things through as he must have had to do. Make no mistake– I consider Robert F. Kennedy to have been one of the most detestable people I've ever heard of, and I would not for a moment try to excuse anything he did. In fact, I can never forgive *John* Kennedy for telling Marilyn the things, in the first place, that got her in trouble, and I can never forgive Bobby Kennedy for the ruthless manner in which he saw to it that Marilyn would remain silent. But I think I *understand* Bobby Kennedy. That is, I think I understand why he regarded himself as no longer having any decent options. He was painted into a corner, and it was his nature that when he was painted into a corner, he wouldn't hesitate to take a wall down to get out of the room if he had to.

Let's imagine what for Bobby would have been the worst-case scenario. From his viewpoint, trying to see into the immediate future, it might have gone something like this.

Marilyn steps in front of the cameras on Monday morning in Los Angeles and says, "The President of the United States has told me an amazing story. Back in 1947 a flying saucer from outer space crashed in New Mexico, and the Army recovered some debris and some little bodies. The bodies weren't human. Jack told me that he had recently gone to a secret place, some Air Force base in Ohio, and had seen the spacecraft and the alien bodies. He said all this is Top Secret, but I think the American people have a right to know about it."

Imagine what would probably happen now.

In seconds, the story goes around the world. The White House is deluged with calls. The President is in a real jam. He can deny the story, but he knows very well that Marilyn Monroe is a popular and credible public person— you don't get a thousand pieces of fan mail a day by being disliked— and he knows that if he denies her account, he can only be digging himself deeper into trouble.

Let us even set aside, for the moment, the stunning revelation that has apparently been made about the government's knowledge of extraterrestrial contact. More immediate, from a political standpoint, is the talk, everywhere from the street corner bar to the halls of Congress, to the effect that Jack Kennedy disclosed *Top Secret* information to someone not authorized to receive it. (At this point the old stories of his affairs with suspected Nazi spy Inga Arvad and various gangland women would surface.) And what does it mean to give away Top Secret information?

The official definition is (and for convenience I quote from Executive Order 12958, but the definition has always been essentially the same):

> "Top Secret" shall be applied to information, the unauthorized disclosure of which reasonably could be expected to cause *exceptionally grave damage to the national security* that the original classification authority is able to identify or describe. [*Emphasis added.*]

The same executive order, in keeping with tradition, defines "national security" as "the national defence or foreign relations of the United States."

Now, one can argue– and I for one certainly *would* argue– that our experiences with crashed UFOs and with extraterrestrial contact *shouldn't* be classified Top Secret. But they are, and always have been, and

90

so the laws apply.

Under these definitions, unauthorized disclosure of Top Secret information can readily be construed as at least potentially aiding the enemies of the United States, especially in times of war or imminent war– and remember, the United States seemed in the summer and fall of 1962 to be poised on the brink of war with Russia over the Cuban missile crisis. In these circumstances, there would be a word for a President's illicit disclosure of Top Secret information.

And the word that would come to mind in high legal circles would be *treason*.

In our imaginary scenario, talk of impeaching the President would soon be echoing through Congress; but even worse, the President would be open to serious criminal charges.

So (following the scenario) Attorney General Robert Kennedy awakes one terrible morning to the realization that his own Department of Justice is going to be prosecuting the President of the United States on charges of treason.

Bobby is going to have to prosecute his brother on charges that could lead not only to deposing him as President, but to sentencing him to prison. (See how ugly all this gets?)

If the President is prosecuted unsuccessfully, without a conviction, everyone will forever say, "Sure, when you're the President and your family is fabulously wealthy and your brother is the Attorney General, you can get away with anything." Even without a conviction, the Presidency goes down the drain at a crucial time when the country appears to be about to go to war and desperately needs solid leadership.

If the President *is* prosecuted successfully, the consequences are not just that he suffers the penalties for treason– the other and more global effect is that it would be very difficult to achieve such a conviction without the government's admitting, at least in the public perception, *that what Marilyn Monroe had described was true.* I.e., to successfully prosecute the President for the probably treasonable act of imparting, to an unauthorized recipient, the Top Secret information that the government has been concealing UFO debris and alien bodies for (at that time) fifteen years, the government would have to admit, in effect, that those things were true. And that, of course, they would never want to admit. It's a classic lose-lose situation.

So on Saturday, August 4, 1962, being an intelligent (if unprincipled) fellow, and having thought all this out, Attorney General Robert Kennedy knows that things are approaching a genuine state of crisis. Marilyn *must not* hold that press conference on Monday morning, because even though she *may* only be planning to tell the world about her affairs with the Kennedy brothers, she may on the other hand be planning to tell the secret of secrets. Bobby can't take the chance, and *must* assume the worst-case scenario. As a last-ditch effort, he goes to Marilyn's house, with Peter Lawford, that Saturday afternoon, and tries to reason with her, tries to get her to behave herself and give up her little red "diary of secrets" and absolutely promise (1) not to hold a press conference and (2) not to bother the Kennedys any more. But instead of finding her mousy and compliant, he finds her hellishly recalcitrant, and he accomplishes nothing more than making her a great deal angrier than she was before. He and his brother-in-law go back to the Lawford beach house for Bobby to think things over.

And when he does, he realizes that the matter is even more desperate, even closer to crisis now than before, because as angry as she is now, Marilyn may not even wait till Monday morning to hold that dreaded press conference, and may well indeed *really* pull all the stops out now, telling even more profound secrets than she had been intending to, prior to Bobby's disgraceful behavior at her house in the afternoon. My suspicion is that Marilyn hadn't really thought all this through– about the probable effects of her "spilling the beans," possibly destroying the Presidency and sending JFK to prison and placing the country in the position of perhaps being at war without well-established leadership– but on that terrible Saturday, Bobby had to assume the worst, and that included assuming that she might tell the *big* secret without wholly realizing what she was doing.

And the Attorney General couldn't let her do that.

So, in this situation, what can Bobby do? Thinking it's now or never, he takes two associates and returns to 12305 Fifth Helena Drive that night after dark, and Marilyn Monroe, at the age of 36, becomes the victim of one of the most heinous crimes ever committed in the name of government secrecy, because she knows that the government has been concealing the remains of a crashed flying saucer.

Marilyn is a classic victim.

If anyone says, "They wouldn't kill anyone to keep things like that secret," I say, "Think again."

And I rest my case.

The evidence speaks for itself. Norma Jeane Mortensen, whom the world knew and loved as Marilyn Monroe, was murdered at the behest of officials of the United States government, and their reasons for doing so were quite literally out of this world.

Recommended Reading

Brown, Peter Harry and Patte B. Barham. *Marilyn: The Last Take.* New York: Signet Books, 1993.

Capell, Frank A. *The Strange Death of Marilyn Monroe.* Staten Island: The Herald of Freedom, 1964.

Greer, Stephen M. *Extraterrestrian Contact: The Evidence and Implications.* Afron, VA: Crossing Point Publications, 1999.

Hesemann, Michael and Philip Mantle. *Beyond Roswell: The Alien Autopsy Film, Area 51, & the U. S. Government Coverup of UFOs.* New York: Marlowe & Company, 1997.

Heymann, C. David. *RFK: A Candid Biography of Robert F. Kennedy.* New York: Dutton Books, 1998.

Maccabee, Bruce. *UFO FBI Connection: The Secret History of the Government's Cover-Up.* St. Paul: Llewellyn Publications, 2000.

Mailer, Norman. *Marilyn: A Biography.* New York: Grosset & Dunlap, 1973.

Randle, Kevid D. *Project Moon Dust: Beyond Roswell– Exposing the Government's Continuing Covert UFO Investigations and Cover-Ups.* New York: Avon Books, 1998.

Slatzer, Robert F. *The Curious Death of Marilyn Monroe.* New York: Pinnacle Books, 1974.

----------. *The Marilyn Files.* New York: S.P.I. Books, 1992.

Speriglio, Milo. *The Marilyn Conspiracy.* New York: Pocket Books, 1986.

Stone, Clifford E. *UFOs are Real: Extraterrestrial Encounters Documented by the U. S. Government.* New York: SPI Books, 1997.

Summers, Anthony. *Goddess: The Secret Lives of Marilyn Monroe.* New York: New American Library, 1985.

Wolfe, Donald H. *The Last Days of Marilyn Monroe.* New York: William Morrow and Company, 1998.